Contents

Designed and created for IMM Lifestyle Books by AG&G Books. Copyright © 2004, 2016 "Specialist" AG&G Books
Design: Glyn Bridgewater; Illustrations: Dawn Brend, Gill Bridgewater and Coral Mula; Editor: Alison Copland; Photographs: see page 80

Current Printing (last digit)
10 9 8 7 6 5 4 3 2 1
Printed in Singapore

Home Gardener's Orchids: Selecting, growing, displaying, improving and maintaining orchids is published by Creative Homeowner under license with IMM Lifestyle Books.

ISBN: 978-1-58011-747-0

Creative Homeowner®, *www.creativehomeowner.com*, is distributed exclusively in North America by Fox Chapel Publishing Company, Inc., 800-457-9112, 1970 Broad Street, East Petersburg, PA 17520 and in the United Kingdom by Grantham Book Service, Trent Road, Grantham, Lincolnshire, NG31 7XQ.

Author's foreword

Orchids are often thought to be difficult to grow and almost impossible for indoor cultivation. In earlier years this was probably accurate, but nowadays it is possible for anyone to grow orchids indoors. However, the major part of such success is in choosing suitable plants. Increasingly, garden centres as well as specialist nurseries sell orchids that are suitable for growing indoors, perhaps on windowsills, tables and in display cabinets. Before creating your own indoor collection, however, it is well worth visiting a few nurseries to see the range of orchids they offer and to make a note of the ones that especially appeal to you.

Orchids can also be grown in greenhouses and heated conservatories, and for this purpose there is an even wider range of suitable plants. Wherever you grow them, their delicate, intricate, colourful and often wax-like nature will enthral you. The orchid family is one of the largest in the plant kingdom, including nearly 800 different genera, more than 25,000 species and in excess of 100,000 man-made hybrids, with many further ones being introduced each year. There are orchids to please just about everyone's taste.

This thoroughly practical, all-colour book guides readers through the plant selection process and the special growing techniques required by orchids, as well as providing an insight into the vast range of orchids that are currently available for growing both indoors and in greenhouses or conservatories.

SPECIALIST NURSERIES

Orchid nurseries often specialize in certain types of orchids. Some concentrate on species orchids, and others on hybrids of selected genera. A glance through a nursery catalogue – or, perhaps, a scroll through relevant websites on the internet – will soon give you an idea of their speciality and range of plants. Do not be deterred from buying from overseas nurseries – many have excellent distribution arrangements as well as agents acting for them in various countries.

About the author

David Squire has a lifetime's experience with plants, both cultivated and native types. He studied botany and gardening at the Hertfordshire College of Horticulture and the Royal Horticultural Society's Garden at Wisley, Surrey. Throughout his gardening and journalistic careers, David has written more than 80 books on plants and gardening, including 14 books in this Specialist Guide series. He also has a wide interest in the uses of native plants, whether for eating and survival, or for their historical roles in medicine, folklore and customs.

From botanical specimens to decorative features

In earlier years, orchids were considered to be colourful, exciting and, perhaps, novel plants that mainly interested botanists. Nowadays, this has radically changed, and suitable ones compete with houseplants as room decorations.
A range of ways to display orchids, either singly or in groups, is described and illustrated on page 15. Many can be grown on windowsills, and suitable types are indicated on page 14. Orchids are even candidates for growing in cabinets and in places where supplementary light has to be provided (see pages 18–19).

What are orchids?

There are two basic types of orchid. *Terrestrial* orchids grow at ground level and are rooted in soil. The other type is *epiphytic* and these grow on trees and shrubs. A few epiphytic orchids grow on debris on rocks, and these are called *lithophytes*. Epiphytic orchids are not parasitical and use their host solely for support and anchorage. They grow in dead plant debris which collects in the angles of branches and provides moisture and nourishment.

Are there many types of orchid?

THE ORCHID FAMILY

Orchids are perennial plants and live from one year to another. Some are herbaceous (their foliage dies down in winter), while others are evergreen. Epiphytic orchids have showier and more flamboyant flowers than terrestrial types, and invariably these are the ones that are primarily grown indoors, as well as in greenhouses and conservatories. The flowers of terrestrial types are less dramatic but nevertheless equally captivating.

The range of orchids is wide but usually restricted to those that can be relatively easily grown. These include Cattleyas, Coelogynes, Cymbidiums, Dendrobiums, Laelias, Lycastes, Miltonias, Odontoglossums, Oncidiums, Paphiopedilums, Phalaenopsis, Pleiones, Stanhopeas, Vandas, Vuylstekearas and Zygopetalums. Members of these families – as well as others – are described and featured on pages 46–77.

Where do orchids come from?

The orchid family is one of the largest in the plant kingdom. Orchids which grow in soil at ground level are usually found in temperate climates, whereas those that grow in crevices and junctions of branches are mainly native to tropical or subtropical regions. The latter invariably enjoy a damp atmosphere, which helps to keep their exposed roots moist, active and pliable.

Dendrobium draconsis *belongs to a large and varied genus of orchids. A number of the species are cultivated, as well as a wide range of colourful and distinctive hybrids.*

Thunia Gattonense, *a well-established epiphytic orchid, has beautiful foliage as well as large and distinctive flowers in summer.*

Specialist orchid nurseries, as well as botanical gardens, create orchid gardens where spectacular displays can be produced. Other humid-loving plants can be grown with them.

What are terrestrial orchids?

How can I recognize terrestrial orchids?

Terrestrial orchids are mainly herbaceous perennials that grow in soil at ground level and have either underground tubers or a tuft of fleshy roots at their base. The leaves are strap-shaped; they range in colour from pale to dark green, and are sometimes spotted or mottled. Several terrestrial orchids are cultivated, but they are usually more difficult to grow than epiphytic types, which have a tropical or subtropical heritage.

WHICH TERRESTRIAL ORCHIDS CAN I GROW?

Most orchids that are grown in greenhouses and conservatories are epiphytes, but there are a few superb terrestrial types to consider. These include the following.

- **Cypripedium orchids** were, in earlier years, recommended for growing in gardens, in rock gardens and beneath deciduous trees. Unfortunately, they are difficult to establish outdoors in cool climates.
- **Paphiopedilum orchids** are mostly terrestrial. They have been widely hybridized and many superb hybrids are now available; most are ideal for growing indoors. Flowers are readily identified by the pouched features at their fronts. Flower colours include yellow, green, brown, violet, purple and deep crimson.
- **Pleione orchids** are terrestrial or semi-epiphytic and in the wild grow on tree trunks and branches, as well as on mossy rocks. In cultivation, some species are grown in cold greenhouses or indoors. Alternatively, in mild areas the hardier types such as *Pleione formosana* can be grown successfully in rock gardens.

Do terrestrial orchids survive lower temperatures than epiphytes?

Because terrestrial orchids are mainly native to temperate regions of the world, they are hardier than the epiphytic types. Some terrestrial orchids can therefore be grown either in cold greenhouses or outdoors in gardens where the temperature does not fall too low in winter.

Paphiopedilum flowers have distinctive pouches at the front, and belong to a genus that has been enthusiastically hybridized. The tiered flowers on the stem in the left picture contrast with the flower of Paphiopedilum primulinum, *on the right.*

Witch factor

It is said that witches used the tubers of terrestrial orchids in their potions and drugs, many of which were planned to influence love. Fresh tubers were said to promote true love, while withered ones were thought to check wrong and ill-advised passions.

Nicholas Culpeper, the English seventeenth-century physician and herbalist, wrote about orchids being under the dominion of Venus.

In addition, bruised orchid tubers were used medicinally in the treatment of certain infections.

CONSERVING NATIVE ORCHIDS

During earlier years, many terrestrial orchids were dug up from their native soil in the wishful belief that they could be transplanted into a garden. Invariably, this resulted in the destruction of many plants. Additionally, many were dug up and pressed as part of a native plant collection.

Several centuries ago, the tuberous and finger-like roots of *Orchis mascula* (Early Purple Orchid) were used to make salop, a drink popular before the introduction of coffee. This resulted in the destruction of many of these orchids, a distinctive plant also known as Dead Men's Fingers and King's Fingers.

Today, it is better to photograph or sketch plants rather than to dig them up, and always take care not to trample on them.

DO TERRESTRIAL ORCHIDS HAVE FRAGRANT FLOWERS?

A few terrestrial orchids have scented flowers; in some, the scent is pleasant, but often it is offensive. Here are some examples.

- *Herminium monorchis* (Musk Orchid) develops small greenish-yellow flowers, and these emit a soft, honey-like fragrance that attracts small bees and beetles.
- *Himantoglossum hircinum* (Lizard Orchid) has flowers that resemble a lizard and emit the rancid smell of stale perspiration akin to goats.
- *Leucorchis albida* or *Pseudorchis albida* (Small White Orchid) has an attractive fragrance, with strongly vanilla-like scent.
- *Orchis mascula* (Early Purple Orchid) has bright purple flowers that when newly opened give off a vanilla scent, but after fertilization this changes to a goat- or cat-like redolence.
- *Orchis ustulata* (Dark-winged Orchid) has flowers with a sweet, almond-like fragrance.

Spiranthes autumnalis *(Autumn Lady's Tresses) emits an almond-like scent.*

WHAT ARE HYBRID ORCHIDS?

Hybrid orchids are man-made plants that have been raised from the crossing of one or more parents. For example, plants in the genus x *Vuylstekeara* are derived from *Cochlioda*, *Miltonia* and *Odontoglossum*. Others, such as x *Laeliocattleya*, are derived from just two genera – *Laelia* and *Cattleya*. Hybrid plants are indicated by a small cross being placed in front of the first name, such as x *Wilsonara*.

Nowadays, most new orchids result from crosses – and back-crosses – with orchids originally introduced from their native countries many decades ago. Refined hybridizing developments have encouraged the creation of new hybrids, and this has been stimulated by greater interest in orchids.

DO ALL ORCHIDS HAVE COMMON NAMES?

Many orchids, including Cattleyas with their distinctive and colourful nature, are ideal for creating corsages.

Epiphytic orchids

Only a few epiphytic orchids have common names, although Cattleyas are often known as Corsage Orchids because of their use in the florist trade (see pages 16–17).

Odontoglossum grande has been dubbed the Tiger Orchid, reflecting the bright yellow petals which are barred chestnut-brown. *Odontoglossum crispum* has been known as the Queen of Orchids on account of its magnificent, sparkling white or pale rose flowers, which are spotted or blotched purple or red. So attractive are the flowers of this plant that the species was nearly brought to extinction in the wild.

Odontoglossum grande *is called the Tiger Orchid because of its striped flowers.*

Terrestrial orchids

Terrestrial orchids are blessed with many highly descriptive local names which invariably refer to the shapes and colours of their flowers. Several members of the *Spiranthes* genus have 'Lady's Tresses' in their names, while the common names of others indicate the type of soil and area in which they grow. These include the Fen Orchid and Meadow Orchid. *Gymnadenia conopsea* is known as the Fragrant Orchid, on account of its flowers being highly scented.

Hardy orchid

Pleione formosana, which is native to a wide area from Tibet to Taiwan (previously called Formosa), is ideal for growing in a cool living room because of its hardiness. Alpine plant enthusiasts have long grown this orchid in alpine greenhouses.

Pleiones are terrestrial or semi-epiphytic orchids; Pleione formosana *is very popular, with many varieties available.*

What are epiphytic orchids?

Do epiphytic orchids grow above the ground?

Epiphytic orchids naturally grow above ground, in crevices and junctions of branches where they gain moisture and food from decaying plant debris which collects in them. They are mainly native to tropical and subtropical regions. These orchids are not parasites, but for their convenience dwell above the ground, with specially adapted roots that serve both to hold them in place and to absorb the moisture and nutrients necessary for survival.

WIDE RANGE OF EPIPHYTIC ORCHIDS

There are many epiphytic orchids but only a relatively few are grown as a hobby in greenhouses or conservatories, and even fewer indoors. Here are a few superb orchids to consider. Together with other orchids, they are described in greater detail in the A–Z of orchids on pages 46–77. Their range of shapes and colours will amaze you.

x *Brassolaeliocattleya*

Hybrids between *Brassovola*, *Laelia* and *Cattleya*, with flowers up to 15 cm (6 in) wide. They can be grown indoors or in greenhouses (see page 48).

Cattleya

Popular orchids, native to a wide area from Mexico to southern Brazil. They are widely grown in greenhouses, as well as indoors (see page 49).

Cirrhopetalum

Evergreen orchids from Africa, Asia and the Pacific Islands. Flowering from mid-spring to early summer, they are best grown in a greenhouse (see page 53).

Coelogyne

Distinctive evergreen orchids from the tropics that often have fragrant flowers and are usually grown in greenhouses (see page 53).

Cymbidium

Easy to grow – some terrestrial and others epiphytic. They are ideal for gardeners new to orchids. Grow in greenhouses or indoors (see page 54).

Dendrobium

Most are deciduous, but those from warm areas are evergreen. Many are easily grown in greenhouses as well as indoors (see page 58).

Epidendrum

A group of New World orchids, mainly deciduous and from Florida to Brazil. Most are easy to grow and ideal for growing in greenhouses (see page 61).

Laelia

New World evergreen orchids native to an area from Mexico to Brazil. They are ideal for growing in greenhouses, as well as indoors (see page 62).

x *Laeliocattleya*

A group of hybrid orchids, between *Laelia* and *Cattleya*. They mainly resemble Cattleyas and are usually grown in greenhouses (see page 62).

Lycaste

Group of tropical, deciduous orchids from Central America. They are ideal for growing in greenhouses as well as indoors (see page 63).

Masdevallia

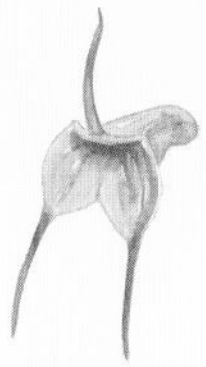

Group of evergreen orchids native to forest areas in the Andes, often known as Kite Orchids because of the long tails to the flowers. They are usually grown in a greenhouse (see page 63).

Maxillaria

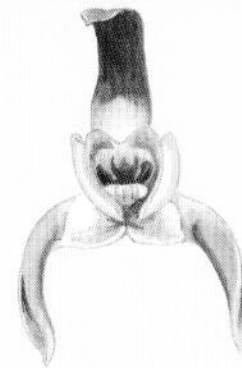

A group of terrestrial and epiphytic evergreen orchids, native to an area from Florida through Central America to Argentina (see page 63).

Miltonia

Distinctive, evergreen orchids from tropical America, some with pansy-like flowers. They are ideal for growing in greenhouses or indoors (see page 64).

Odontoglossum

Popular evergreen orchids, native to Central America and tropical South America, grown in greenhouses as well as indoors (see page 67).

Oncidium

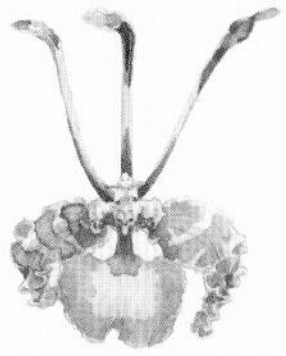

Large group of evergreen orchids, native to the American subtropics. They are ideal for growing in greenhouses as well as indoors (see page 68).

Phalaenopsis

Evergreen orchids, native to a wide area from India and Indonesia to the Philippines and northern Australia. They are often grown in greenhouses as well as indoors (see page 70).

x *Sophrolaeliocattleya*

Group of hybrid orchids that are derived from *Cattleya*, *Laelia* and *Sophronitis*, which mainly resemble Cattleyas (see page 74).

Stanhopea

Evergreen orchids native to Central America, the American tropics and Mexico, usually grown in greenhouses as well as indoors (see page 74).

Vanda

Popular group of evergreen orchids native to tropical Asia. They are grown in greenhouses as well as indoors (see page 75).

x *Vuylstekeara*

Group of hybrid orchids, derived from *Cochlioda*, *Miltonia* and *Odontoglossum*. They mainly bear a resemblance to Odontoglossums. They are grown in greenhouses or indoors (see page 76).

Zygopetalum

Evergreen orchids from Brazil, Venezuela, Colombia and the Guianas. They can be grown in greenhouses as well as indoors (see page 77).

Orchidomania

When did orchids become popular?

Records indicate that the Greek thinker and writer Theophrastus, born about 370 BC and a friend of Aristotle and Plato, referred to a group of plants known as 'orchis' on account of the large, rounded, testicular tubers borne in pairs at the bases of many terrestrial orchids (the Greek for testis is *orchis*). During the early 1700s, the church, trading companies and botanists ventured into foreign countries, returning with plants, some of them orchids.

CHANCE PLAYS A ROLE

By 1789, there were about 15 exotic orchid species growing in Britain and Cattleyas were being regularly flowered during the second decade of the 1800s. However, by chance and at about the same time, a consignment of tropical plants wrapped in other tough plants was sent to the North London gardener William Cattley, who was a tropical plant enthusiast (his name is now remembered in the genus *Cattleya*).

Many orchids were bred by the Veitch Nursery, producing the first man-made orchid hybrid in 1856. This illustration shows a two-year old orchid seedling.

This delicate illustration of Cypripedium parviflorum *(Yellow Ladies Slipper) was drawn by S. Edwards in 1820. It flowers from mid-spring to mid-summer and is now better known as* Cypripedium calceolus *var.* parviflorum. *In North America it is called Small Golden Slipper.*

Cattley was intrigued by the wrapping material and by late 1818 he had encouraged it to bear flowers that caused a sensation in the plant world. Nothing like it had been known in cultivation, and before long a mania for orchids had begun in Britain, Europe and North America, but at a dreadful cost for orchids in the wild where whole areas were cleared of orchids. Trees were felled in order to get at orchids growing at their tops, and land was denuded of plants to prevent competitors laying hands on them. It was of no credit to horticulture and reveals how depraved people are when money is the dictum. Nevertheless, new species of orchid flooded into Europe.

Many new plant nurseries came into business, some sending out collectors to tropical and subtropical regions. Towards the end of the 1890s, the cost of maintaining a collector abroad was about £3,000 a year, and some firms had upwards of 20 collectors. This cost was reflected in the expense of growing orchids, which mainly became a pursuit of the wealthy.

THE INTRODUCTION OF HYBRIDS

Above: x Beallara *Peggy Ruth has a dominant appearance, with clear markings on its petals. There are several closely related hybrids. Left: The large, frilly, pink petals of this Odontoglossum hybrid create a dramatic feature.*

The technique of creating hybrids was discovered about the mid-1800s and the first man-made hybrids were crosses between *Calanthe furcata* and *Calanthe masuca*, with flowering in 1856. However, it is known that natural hybrids had occurred earlier. Nowadays, many hybrids are the result of crosses between two or three different genera – sometimes more – and these are acknowledged by putting an x before the name. A look through an orchid catalogue soon reveals the wealth of hybrids.

EARLY AMERICAN ORCHID COLLECTORS

Epiphytic orchids, earlier sent to Britain from tropical areas, were despatched from Britain to North America in the late 1830s, with a collection being sent to John Boott, who lived in Massachusetts.

Later, in 1865, the orchid collection of Edward Rand was presented to Harvard University, where it eventually developed into a major North American collection.

Was vanilla first obtained from an orchid?

The warm, luxurious bouquet and flavour of vanilla was originally derived from pods produced by the large, creeping orchid *Vanilla planifolia*, native to Central America and used by the Aztecs many years before Christopher Columbus chanced upon their shores in the late fifteenth century.

A related orchid, *Vanilla pompona*, also known as Vanillon or Vanilloes, produces inferior-quality vanilla, although it is said to have advantages over *Vanilla planifolia* as the pods are thicker and shorter and not so likely to split at their ends.

Nowadays, the flavouring agent vanillin is produced synthetically for use in commercial confectionery, by perfumers and for scenting tobacco.

HAVE ORCHIDS BEEN USED MEDICINALLY?

During the early sixteenth century, the *Doctorine of Signatures* (a development of mimetic magic or like-suggesting-like), which had been known for more than a thousand years, was popularized by the Swiss-German physician and alchemist Philippus Aureolus Paracelsus (1493–1541). He suggested that the medicinal value of any natural substance is indicated by its nature, such as size, shape and colour. This was thought to be the stamp of a guardian angel. Because the tuberous roots of many terrestrial orchids resembled testicles, it was thought that crushing and eating the tubers would stimulate sexual activity. Additionally, the nectar of the terrestrial *Orchis mascula* when squeezed into goat's milk was said by John Partridge, physician to Charles I, to 'excite both sexes'.

A depiction of Orchis, featured in the 1597 Herball *of John Gerard, an enthusiastic botanist and barber-surgeon in London, mainly during the late 1500s.*

Orchid flowers

What is the structure of orchid flowers?

In size, orchid flowers range from minute types to ones 20 cm (8 in) across. Even within a genus, the shapes and sizes of flowers also vary widely. However, all orchid flowers have the same basic form, irrespective of whether they are borne singly on a stem, such as with *Pleione formosana* (although some have two flowers on a stem), or in clusters on pendulous stems, like those of *Dendrobium densiflorum*. Each flower has three petals and three sepals.

FLOWER STRUCTURE

Orchids are invariably grown for their attractive flowers, which, although having the same basic structure, are extremely diverse in size and colour.

The outermost parts of an orchid flower are the three sepals, which in most non-orchid flowers are green and help to protect the flower when it is still at its bud stage. Typically, these are the green, tough segments seen around the buds of roses. In orchids, however, they are coloured and help to create greater colour and size. The uppermost sepal in each flower – known as the dorsal sepal – is slightly larger than the other two, which are positioned at each side and towards the base of the flower. The size and shape of these sepals varies greatly from species to species, and plant breeders have developed orchids that have larger and more distinctive sepals.

Each orchid flower also has three petals and these are coloured. The two uppermost petals, on either side of the flower, are equal in size and shape. However, the lower one is usually formed into the shape of a lip and known as the labellum. This lower petal is the most ornamental and elaborately formed of all the flower parts on an orchid and frequently acts as a landing platform for pollinating insects. Also, in colour and shape it often mimics insects, thereby attracting them to the flower.

↘ *Few flowers are as colourful and intricately shaped as those of orchids. They have evolved into many shapes, but all with the same basic parts.*

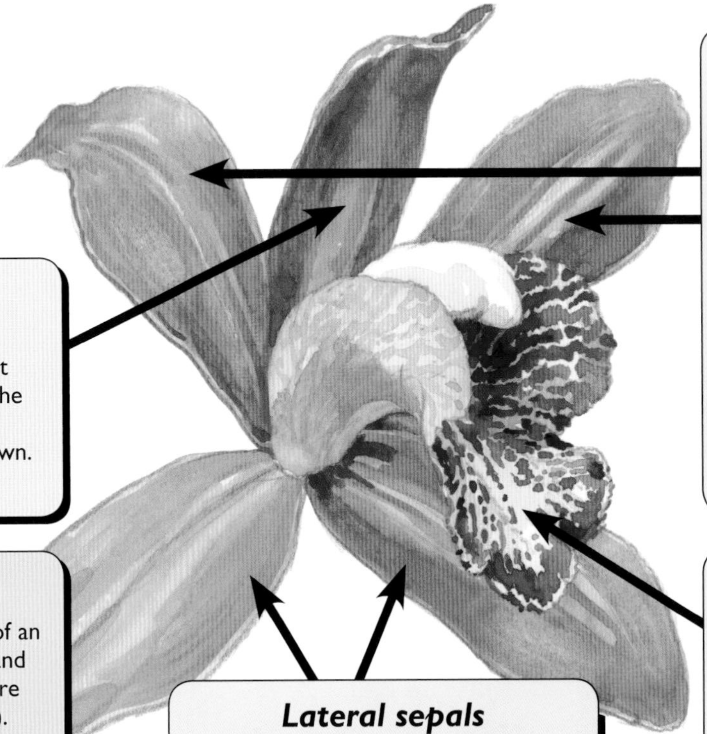

Upper petals

Two equally sized petals are positioned on either side of the flower and towards the top or middle. Like all other parts of an orchid flower, the upper petals vary in size and shape. In some flowers they are narrow and slightly drooping; in others they are wide and horizontal, creating a dramatic background for the lip (labellum).

Dorsal sepal

This is the uppermost sepal and in size the most dominant of the three. The other two sepals are on either side and lower down.

Column

The reproductive parts of an orchid are at its centre and have a finger-like structure (hence the term column). The majority of orchid flowers are bisexual, with both the female and male reproductive parts present on each flower.

Lateral sepals

On either side and towards the base of the flower are two equally sized sepals. These are coloured, and their size and shape varies from species to species.

Lip

The lip (or labellum) is the lower petal and the most spectacular part of an orchid flower. It various enormously in shape and size. In some orchids, it forms a distinctive pouch, while in others it is flat or dished. Its shape is ideal for visiting insects.

Flower variations

The shapes of flowers differ slightly but basically they have the same construction. Here are examples that reveal the different but similar parts.

Cattleya

Corsage Orchid, with magnificent, waxy flowers 10–15 cm (4–6 in) across.

Miltonia

Often known as the Pansy Orchid, with pansy-like flowers 5–10 cm (2–4 in) across.

Odontoglossum

Usually circular, large flowers borne in spikes of 8–10 flowers.

Paphiopedilum

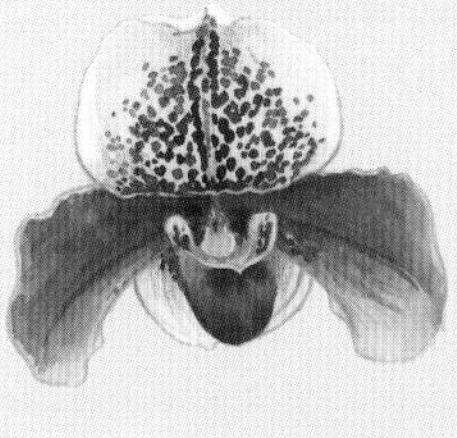

Widely known as the Slipper Orchid, with distinctively pouched flowers.

Phalaenopsis

The Moth Orchid, with rounded and usually flattish flowers, 5 cm (2 in) across.

Dendrobium

Brightly coloured flowers, 3.5 cm (1½ in) across, borne in erect or pendent spikes.

Paphiopedilum orchids are descriptively known as Slipper Orchids because of their distinctive pouch-shaped lips, which distinguish them from other orchids.

SCENT COLOUR AND SHAPE

Scent, as well as the colour and shape of an orchid flower, attracts pollinating insects. Throughout the plant world, scent is important in attracting a pollinator.

- **Scent:** this varies according to the type of insect a flower wishes to lure. For example, where flowers are pollinated by moths the fragrance is usually absent in daylight hours, but evident during the evening and into the night when many moths are flying. The range of scents emitted by flowers varies, and although many are sweet those of some tropical orchids, which are pollinated by flies, have the redolence of carrion and are distinctively unpleasant.
- **Colour:** flowers that are pollinated during the day invariably have highly coloured petals, whereas those pollinated at night are usually bland and often a glistening white to create a well-defined shape.
- **Shape:** to entice suitable pollinating insects, some orchid flowers resemble the desired insect. This is known as mimicry and encompasses flowers which have parts that resemble bees, wasps and spiders.

VERTICAL SYMMETRY

Despite the fact that the flowers of orchids vary from one species to another, each flower can always be divided vertically into two equal halves.

FLOWERING ARRANGEMENTS

Some orchids bear flowers singly or in small groups and, perhaps, on upright stems. Others have arching stems with pendulous clusters formed of many separate flowers. The flowering nature often indicates how plants are best grown; those with single and upright stems are usually grown in pots, whereas those with cascading and arching stems are ideal for planting in baskets, or in pots positioned towards the edge of a shelf.

Comparettia *is a small but interesting genus – the plants produce drooping flower stems that are peppered with distinctive flowers.*

The anatomy of orchids

What is the structure of an orchid?

Orchids grow in two main ways. Some are terrestrial and flourish in soil at ground level, while others are epiphytic and in the wild gain support from trees and shrubs. A few also grow on rocks. Some epiphytes have monopodial growth, while others are sympodial (see opposite page for details and illustrations). Additionally, they have variably shaped pseudobulbs and different root structures (see opposite page).

STRUCTURE OF AN EPIPHYTIC ORCHID

The majority of orchids grown by orchid hobbyists are epiphytes. Terrestrial types have different root systems (fleshy-rooted or tuberous) and these are explained and illustrated on the opposite page. Here are the main parts of an epiphytic orchid.

Flowers

Flowers grow on stalks which mostly develop from the top of a pseudobulb (see right). Some flowers are borne solitarily, others in clusters on stems which sometimes arch or trail.

Leaves

Leaves are usually thick and leathery and able to support themselves in an upright or arching stance. They grow from the top of the pseudobulb and are able to use sunshine, together with water and nutrients absorbed by the orchid's roots, to create growth.

Backbulbs

Backbulbs are old pseudobulbs (for function and description, see right) and remain after flowers fade and die. Backbulbs remain at the base of some orchids for several years, and are usually removed when a plant is repotted (see pages 38–39).

Pseudobulbs

Pseudobulbs are the thickened bases of stems and are able to store moisture and food. It is from pseudobulbs that flower stalks mainly arise. Pseudobulbs vary in size and shape and they help identify orchids (see opposite page). Some orchids, such as Vandas, do not have pseudobulbs.

Roots

Roots arise from the bases of pseudobulbs or a rhizome, which in orchids is a thickened, horizontal underground stem. The roots are usually thick and both absorb and store moisture. Additionally, they anchor the orchid to a tree in the wild or, when cultivated, in a container. Increasingly, many epiphytic orchids are grown in transparent plastic pots.

Bulbophyllum orchids are epiphytic, with flowers that are produced either singly or in a cluster or rosette.

Some orchids bear their flowers on long stems – sometimes arching or cascading – making them ideal for growing in a basket.

PATTERNS OF GROWTH

Technically, epiphytic orchids have two basic patterns of growth. They are either monopodial or sympodial. The majority of orchids have sympodial growth.

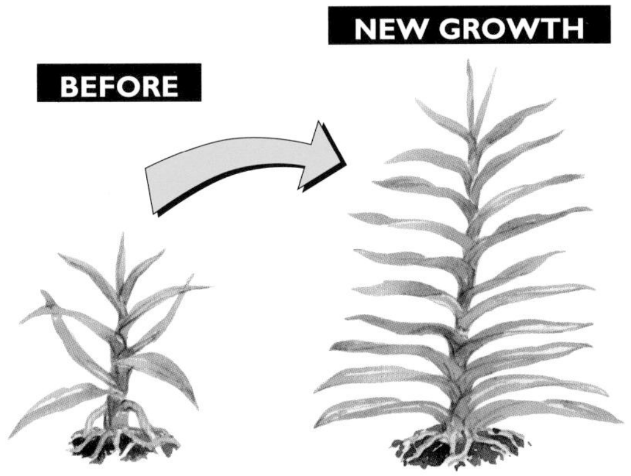

Monopodial orchids

These create growth mainly upwards, with new growth being an extension of growth produced during earlier years. They develop leaves on either side of a central stem.

A few monopodial orchids are exceptionally vigorous and not suitable for greenhouse or indoor cultivation, but Phalaenopsis are popular and widely available for sale at nurseries and garden centres. Vandas are other monopodial orchids and often seen in orchid collections.

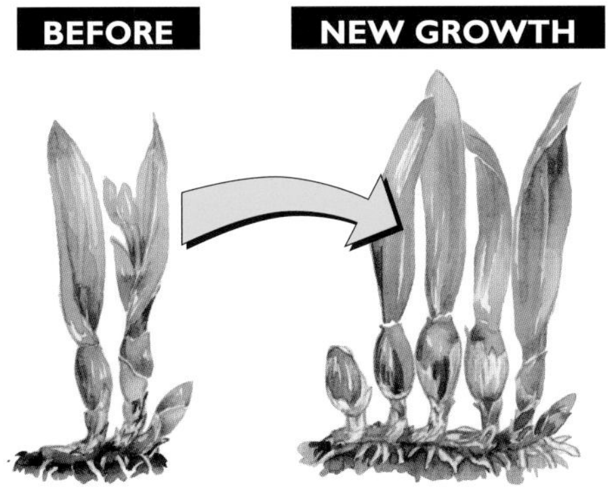

Sympodial orchids

These develop new growth from the base of the previous growth. Many sympodial orchids have pseudobulbs, which are thickenings at the base of a stem. However, some sympodial orchids do not have pseudobulbs and these types are mainly native to areas where there is a regular and constant supply of moisture.

There are many types of pseudobulbs and all sympodial orchids create new growth from the base of the previous ones. Examples of pseudobulbs are illustrated below.

ROOTS AND PSEUDOBULBS

Similar to the roots of other plants, those of orchids anchor the plant and are a means of absorbing moisture and food. There are several types of roots. The roots of epiphytic orchids arise from their pseudobulbs (see below). The roots of terrestrial orchids do not arise from pseudobulbs; instead, they are either spherical tubers with fine roots, or clusters of fleshy roots. The roots of terrestrial orchids in warm climates are thicker than those plants in temperate climates. The tubers of terrestrial orchids especially enable plants to survive periods of cold and dry weather, with a later resurgence in growth when conditions are right.

Three types of pseudobulbs on epiphytic orchids

➚ Small, thin, almost cane-like pseudobulbs (as in Dendrobiums).

➚ Flattened or slightly rounded pseudobulbs (as in Oncidiums).

➚ Elongated or club-shaped pseudobulbs (as in Cattleyas).

Tuberous roots on a terrestrial orchid

🡐 Some terrestrial orchids, such as the popular Ophrys apiferea *(Bee Orchid), have two spherical tubers and fine roots.*

Are orchids evergreen?

Some orchids are evergreen, especially those that are native to tropical regions where growth continues throughout the year. Others are herbaceous. The nature of many orchids is indicated in the A–Z of orchids on pages 46–77.

Indoor orchids

Can orchids be grown indoors?

Nowadays, there is a wide range of orchids, and the major factor for success when growing them indoors is to select suitable plants. Indoor orchids are widely sold by garden centres and specialist orchid nurseries. The other element in successful indoor cultivation is not to have high temperatures and a stuffy atmosphere. Good ventilation is essential, but avoid cold draughts from windows near plants (see pages 20–27 for specific details on growing orchids indoors).

Many Phalaenopsis orchids can be grown indoors. The flowers are long-lasting and some can be positioned on a windowsill.

Displaying and growing indoor orchids

In pots indoors – *see page 15*

Essential tips for display – *see page 16*

Creating corsages and buttonholes – *see pages 16–17*

In growing-cases – *see page 18*

In cellars and attics – *see page 19*

How to grow indoor orchids:

- Cymbidiums – *see page 20*
- Miltonias – *see page 21*
- Odontoglossums – *see page 22*
- Paphiopedilums – *see page 23*
- Phalaenopsis – *see page 24*
- Zygopetalums – *see page 25*

Other indoor orchids – *see pages 26–27*

ORCHIDS FOR GROWING ON WINDOWSILLS

- *Aspasia lunata* (see page 47)
- *Brassia memoria* Fritz Boedeker (see page 47)
- *Brassia* Rising Star (see page 47)
- *Brassia verrucosa* (see page 48)
- *Coelogyne cristata* (see page 53)
- *Coelogyne fimbriata* (see page 53)
- *Coelogyne flaccida* (see page 53)
- *Coelogyne memoria* William Micholtz 'Burnham' (see page 54)
- *Coelogyne ochracea* (see page 54)
- *Dendrobium farmeri* (see page 58)
- *Dendrobium nobile* (see page 59)
- *Encyclia cochleata* (see page 60)
- *Encyclia lancifolia* (see page 60)
- *Encyclia radiata* (see page 60)
- *Laelia anceps* (see page 62)
- *Maxillaria hematoglossa* (see page 64)
- *Maxillaria praestans* (see page 64)
- *Maxillaria tenuifolia* 'Yellow' (see page 64)
- *Miltonia clowesii* (see page 64)
- *Miltonia spectabilis* (see page 64)
- *Miltoniopsis* Anjou (see page 65)
- *Miltoniopsis* Herr Alexandre (see page 65)
- *Miltoniopsis* Hudson Bay (see page 65)
- *Miltoniopsis* Saint Helier (see page 66)
- *Odontoglossum* Geyser Gold (see page 67)
- *Oncidium ornithorhynchum* (see page 68)
- *Oncidum* Splinter 'Norman' (see page 68)
- *Oncidium* Star Wars (see page 69)
- *Paphiopedilum* Delophyllum (see page 69)
- *Phalaenopsis* Cool Breeze (see page 70)
- *Phalaenopsis* Follet (see page 70)
- *Phalaenopsis* Pink Twilight (see page 73)
- *Phalaenopsis* Yellow Treasure (see page 70)
- *Pleione formosana* (see page 74)
- *Pleione shantung* 'Ridgeway' (see page 74)
- x *Vuylstekeara* Cambria 'Plush' (see page 77)

WHERE CAN I GROW ORCHIDS INDOORS?

There are many places in which orchids can be displayed indoors, including windowsills, table-tops, wall-mounted brackets, growing-cases and ornamental half-barrels placed on the floor. Here are few places to consider.

On windowsills

↘ Orchids must not be exposed to direct sunlight, and therefore net curtains are useful for diffusing strong light. Stand each individual pot in shallow tray with a 2.5 cm (1 in) thick layer of gravel or clay granules in its base. Keep this layer moist but not waterlogged. It both keeps the compost and roots cool and creates a level of humidity around the plants.

Single-pot displays

↙ These create distinctive displays on windowsills and tables. Choose a pot that will complement in colour the orchid's flowers; additionally, add a colour-harmonizing saucer to prevent moisture escaping and trickling onto painted or varnished surfaces. Cover the top of the compost with attractive pebbles.

Wall-mounted brackets

↗ These can be used to display orchids in pots – but choose small types with stems that do not arch and cascade too far. Additionally, try to harmonize the colour of the orchid's flowers with the wall covering. Check that there is a saucer in the wall-bracket's base that will prevent water dribbling out of the display and down the wall if an excessive amount of water is given to a plant.

Shallow ornamental dish on a table

↗ Choose an attractive, wide-based tray and line it with polythene so that initially it rises about 5 cm (2 in) above the rim. Add a 2.5 cm (1 in) thick layer of gravel or clay granules to its base. This needs to be kept constantly moist but should not be waterlogged. Again trim the polythene, but this time so that it is slightly below the container's rim. Stand the pots in position and scatter small wood-chippings around them to create a decorative surface.

Groups of pots

↘ Groups of three of more orchids, each in an attractive pot and in a variety of sizes and shapes, will create eye-pleasing features on tables. For added interest – and to protect the surface of the table – try placing the group of pots in a round, shallow, ornate tray. When displaying orchids in groups, choose either three or five plants, because odd numbers of containers are always easier to arrange than those in even-numbered arrangements.

In ornate half-barrels

← These are made of varnished wood and supported on three or four legs, so that the rim of the feature is about 45 cm (18 in) above the ground. Position a piece of polythene in the container's base and up the inside of the sides. Then, place a 5 cm (2 in) thick layer of either shingle or clay granules in the base. When moist, but not waterlogged, this will help to keep the compost cool as well as creating humidity around the plants. Trim the polythene slightly below the tops of the containers, then stand the pots of orchids in the base.

Displaying orchids indoors

Should I grow indoor or greenhouse orchids?

Many superb orchids can be grown indoors, whereas others are better grown in greenhouses and taken indoors when in flower. Some specialist orchid nurseries will look after your orchids when they are not in flower, and then return them to you to enjoy for the duration of their flowering period. This arrangement is ideal for orchid enthusiasts who live in flats, or where limited garden space prevents the construction of a greenhouse.

ESSENTIAL TIPS FOR DISPLAYING INDOOR ORCHIDS

- Create humidity around plants by placing them on gravel or clay granules in a tray; keep them moist but without any risk of waterlogging the compost.
- Do not position plants in draughts, in direct sunlight or near hot fires. During the summertime only, empty hearth areas around fires make cool and usually slightly shaded homes for orchids, but such positions should not be too dark and gloomy.
- Do not place orchids on unshaded windowsills: in summer, direct and strong sunlight will damage them.
- In winter, take care that orchids will not be trapped between a cold window and a curtain. Also, heavy curtains may knock and damage plants and flowers.
- Check plants daily to ensure that the compost is moist. Watering is best done by taking plants into a kitchen or bathroom and watering over the rim.
- Do not position orchids where they can be knocked by boisterous children or become vulnerable to the frolics of dogs. The tail of a large dog – especially a labrador – can be a lethal weapon to orchids!

CREATING AN ATTRACTIVE INDOOR DISPLAY

Transparent containers will introduce novelty to a display of indoor orchids.

Corsages and buttonholes

Some of the most simple yet stunningly attractive corsages and buttonholes can be created from orchids such as Dendrobiums and Phalaenopsis, with the addition of foliage from widely grown houseplants. Ideal foliage plants include the following:

- *Adiantum raddianum* (Delta Maidenhair Fern; also known as *Adiantum cuneatum*): evergreen fern with dainty, arching fronds.
- *Chlorophytum comosum* 'Variegatum' (Spider Plant): evergreen houseplant with long, tapering leaves with green leaves edged in white. The variety 'Vittatum' is also attractive.
- Small-leaved variegated *Hedera helix* (Ivies): do not use the large-leaved types because they are too dominant.
- *Pilea cadieri* (Aluminium Plant): evergreen houseplant with quilted, dark leaves that have silvery patches.
- *Sedum sieboldii* 'Medio-variegatum': distinctive succulent houseplant with somewhat circular, cream-coloured leaves edged in blue-green. Use this plant reservedly, because otherwise it can be too dominant in corsages.

Adiantum raddianum

Pilea cadieri

Chlorophytum comosum 'Variegatum'

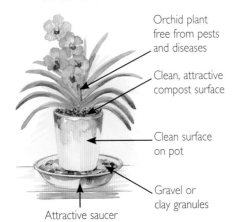

Sedum sieboldii 'Mediovariegatum'

STEP BY STEP TO CREATE A CORSAGE

Creating a corsage from your own orchid flowers and a few leaves from houseplants produces an exciting display.

1 *Place the cut stems – longer than needed – in water overnight. This ensures that stems and flowers are firm and will last a long time when displayed. Corsages can be formed from one or three orchid flowers. It is more difficult to arrange two flowers attractively than one or three.*

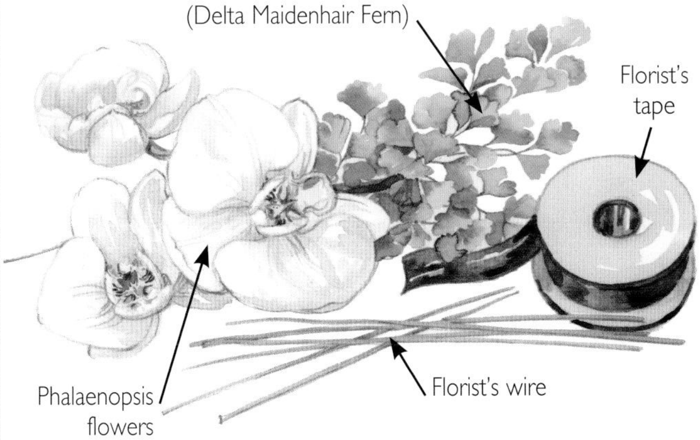

2 *Before forming the corsage, collect together all of the material needed, such as florist's wire and dark green tape, as well as a few leaves from other plants (see left) that will create colour and shape contrasts to the orchid flowers.*

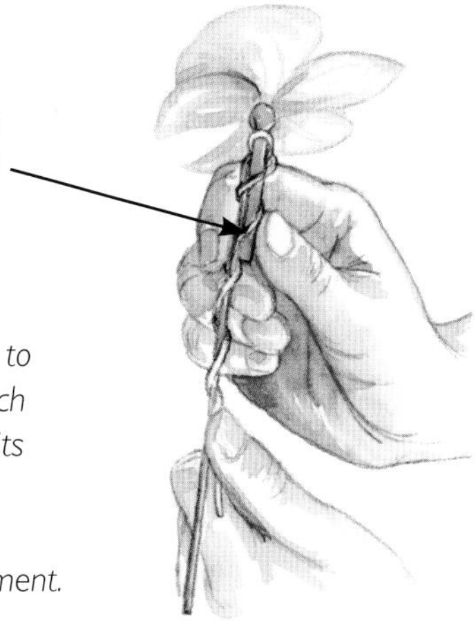

3 *The first stage of assembling the corsage is to add a piece of wire to each orchid's stem to increase its length, give it rigidity and to ensure that it is easily positioned in the arrangement.*

4 *Cover the wire and stem with dark green florist's tape (although other colours can be used, they should be demure and not dominate the arrangement). If three orchid flowers are used, wire them separately.*

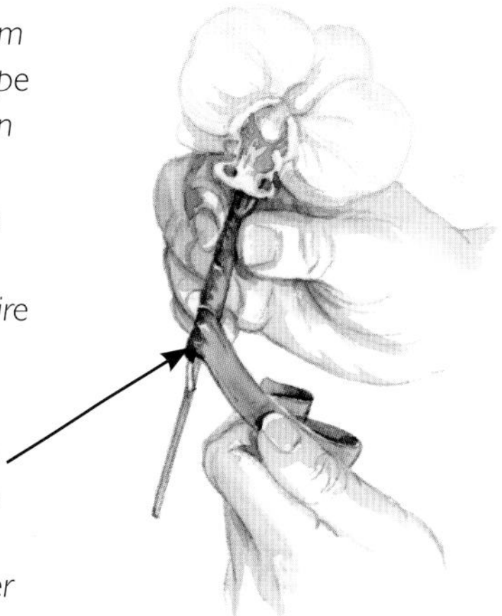

5 *If only one orchid flower is used, add the foliage to the back of the orchid and tape them in position. If three orchids are used, the edges of the flowers should slightly overlap each other.*

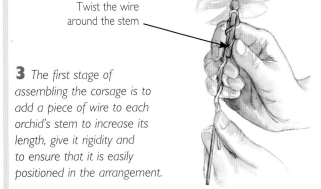

Keeping corsages and buttonholes fresh

Buttonholes and corsages often have to be made up a day or so before they are needed.

If this is the case, complete the arrangement, put it in a plastic box and place it in a refrigerator, where it will remain in good condition for several days.

CAN ORCHIDS BE DISPLAYED IN VASES?

Orchid flowers, when cut and displayed indoors, will captivate you for many weeks. Before cutting the stem, wait until the terminal flower has been open for about eight days. (Incidentally, the flowers when cut will last just as long off the plant as they would have if left on it.) The plant is then able to put all of its energies into growth and the creation of an even better display of flowers during the following year.

TIPS FOR SUCCESS

After cutting the stem of an orchid that is to be displayed indoors, immediately place it in clean water. Top up the water daily. Every few days, cut off a thin slice from the base of the stem – at a slight angle – and renew the water. Take care not to crush the stem, as this reduces its ability to absorb water.

Orchids in growing-cases

What are growing-cases?

Growing-cases are ornate, miniature greenhouses that can be used indoors, both as display features and places in which orchids can be grown. They are usually about 1.8 m (6 ft) high, 1.5–1.8 m (5–6 ft) long and 60 cm (2 ft) deep, and made out of a wooden or metal framework and large, plate-glass sides and front. Growing-cases are usually constructed on strong legs 20–25 cm (8–10 in) high. Orchids may also be grown in old fish or reptile tanks, as well as in cellars.

ANATOMY OF A GROWING-CASE

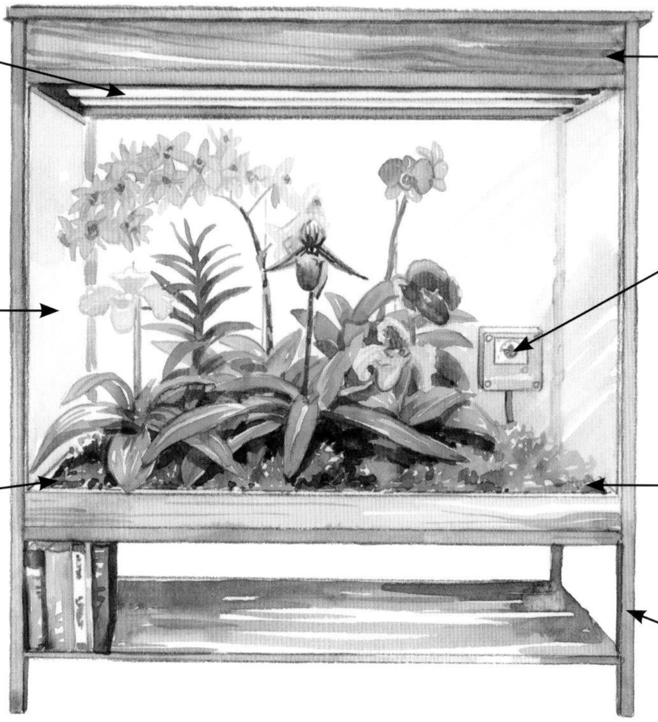

Growth-inducing fluorescent tube lights recessed into the top of the growing-case. It is essential to have 'cool' lights, as otherwise the temperature rises dramatically.
Use plate glass, rather than thin greenhouse or window glass. This makes it a great deal safer for young children as well as adults.
Decorative gravel tray in which the pots of orchids are wholly or partly plunged (for a range of suitable orchids, see below). This helps to keep the compost moist and cool. Use moisture-retentive materials such as clay granules or gravel.
Ventilation is essential, both for fresh air to enter at the base of the growing-case and for hot air to escape at the top.
Thermostat to ensure that the temperature is suitable and that it is lower at night than during the day. Have all electrical equipment installed by a competent electrician.
Gravel or clay granules, several centimetres deep.
Strong legs keep the growing case off the floor and create a display place for books.

Orchids for growing-cases

Several orchids can be grown in growing-cases, and in general they are low-light and cool-growing types. Here are a few orchids to consider:

- *Brassia verrucosa*
- x *Brassolaeliocatteya* 'Norman's Bay'
- *Cattleya aurantiaca*
- Paphiopedilums – there are many that are suitable, and a selection is given on pages 69–70.
- Phalaenopsis – there are many that are suitable, and a wide selection is given on pages 70–73.

An indoor growing-case (sometimes called an indoor greenhouse) creates an ideal home for many orchids.

Orchids in small displays

Displays of orchids need not be large and dominant to be attractive. Instead, small orchids can be grown in an old fish tank (aquarium) – see opposite page – or reptile tank (vivarium), or even in an old and small glass-sided display case.

Car-boot or garage sales are good places to look for novel but practical containers for orchids.

CREATING A DISPLAY IN A FISH TANK (AQUARIUM)

1 Choose a strong aquarium and use a scrubbing brush and detergent to clean it thoroughly. Then wash it with clean water until all traces of detergent have gone. Check that it does not leak.

2 Allow it to dry, and if large place in its display position. Ensure that polished surfaces will not be damaged. Choose a slightly shaded position; avoid windowsills and other places in strong sunlight.

3 Spread expanded clay pellets in the base to a depth of about 2.5 cm (1 in). Place a few ornamental rocks on the base and put in a few orchids, still in their pots. The addition of a few pots of small indoor ferns will enhance the display. Then spread moist sphagnum moss around and slightly over the pots so that they cannot be seen.

GROWING ORCHIDS IN CELLARS

Even cellars (and attics) offer homes for orchids if heating and artificial lighting can be installed. Clearly, the installation does not have to be as decorative as a growing-case in a living room. An electrical power supply is essential; you must have it checked by a competent electrician, especially if the cellar is known to be slightly damp.

Fluorescent lighting tubes can be fitted within a decorative frame and suspended about 30 cm (1 ft) above the tops of the orchids. These enable the orchids to grow all year round; a cycle of 16 hours with the light on followed by 8 hours of darkness produces vigorous growth throughout the year.

Additionally, a temperature of 21°C (70°F) will ensure active growth. Tubular electrical heating tubes can be used, with the addition of a electrical fan to circulate the air gently and thereby prevent the build-up of high temperatures. Thermostats are essential in order to control the temperature.

WATERING

Leaving the plants in their pots makes it possible to water them individually. Fold back the sphagnum moss and check the compost in each pot. After watering, replace the moss.

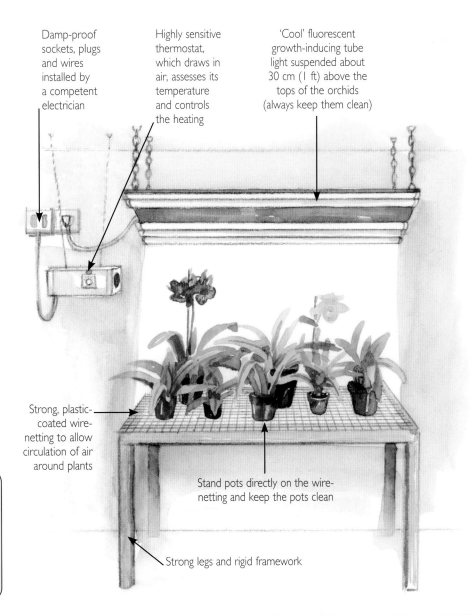

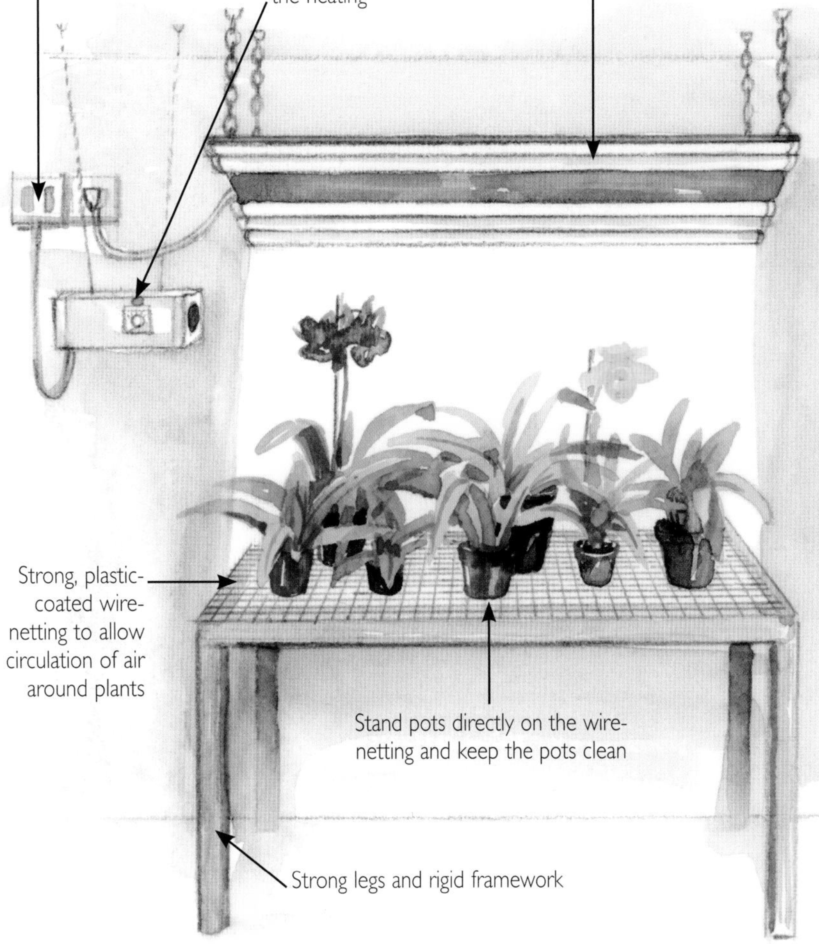

How to grow indoor orchids

Do all indoor orchids need the same treatment?

Orchids are variable plants in their needs and what suits one of them may not be right for another. Some orchids – such as Cymbidiums, Miltonias, Odontoglossums, Paphiopedilums, Phalaenopsis and Zygopetalums – are widely grown indoors, and there is specific advice about growing them here and on the following few pages. If, however, you have an indoor orchid which is not in these groups, the cultural information on pages 26–27 will be invaluable.

SUCCESS WITH SIX DIFFERENT GROUPS OF INDOOR ORCHIDS

A GUIDE TO GROWING CYMBIDIUMS

Superb orchids, with modern ones in a wide colour range and spikes that bear 6–20 long-lasting flowers. Large-flowered types (also known as Standard Cymbidiums) normally flower from early winter to late spring, with flowers lasting 8–12 weeks. Miniature types flower from mid-autumn to late spring, with flowers lasting 6–8 weeks and sometimes longer.

Temperature

- At night: 11–14°F (52–57°F)
- During the day: 16–20°C (61–68°F)

Warning: Cymbidiums do not like high temperatures, so ensure that sufficient ventilation is available. Additionally, when flower buds are developing it is essential that the temperature at night falls below 15°C (59°F).

Position

- From the latter part of early autumn through to late spring, give your orchid plenty of light.
- From the latter part of early summer to early autumn, place your orchid in moderate to good light outside or in a cold greenhouse. However, ensure that direct and strong sunlight cannot reach it at the height of summer.
- Slowly acclimatize plants to outdoor or cool greenhouse conditions in early summer, and slowly to indoor conditions in early autumn.

Watering

- The frequency of watering is influenced by the time of year and where the plant is positioned. Keep the compost evenly moist but not waterlogged, and remember that although the surface may appear dry the base could be moist. The type of compost influences the frequency of watering.

➔ Cymbidium *Baltic Ballet 'Aida' has pink petals and a distinctive, waxy sheen.*

Humidity

- To ensure humidity around the plant, stand it on moist gravel. However, ensure that the base of the pot is not constantly soaked.

Feeding

- Add a specific orchid fertilizer to the watering water. However, omit the fertilizer at every third or fourth watering.
- Always use a proprietary orchid fertilizer and do not exceed the manufacturer's recommended concentration or frequency rate. When used excessively and in strong concentrations, fertilizers can damage the roots of an orchid.
- Do not feed orchids that are in poor condition until they have developed a healthy and large root system.

Repotting and compost

- Repot your orchid directly after flowering, usually every 2–3 years. Free-draining compost is essential, formed of two parts fibrous peat (with a pH of 6.2) and one part coarse perlite. It is also possible to add bark to the mixture.
- See page 37 for other suitable compost mixtures.

Supporting

- Use unobtrusive, strong but thin, canes to support flower spikes. After flowering, remove the canes and cut the stem to 5 cm (2 in) high.

A GUIDE TO GROWING MILTONIAS

Miltonia *Saint Helier 'Red Jewel' creates a fine display with its red flowers.*

Position orchids that prefer diffused light on tables – but avoid dark areas.

Widely known as Pansy Orchids because of the likeness of their flowers to those of garden pansies, these epiphytic and often fragrant orchids create magnificent displays indoors. Miltonias flower at various times of the year but chiefly in late spring or early summer. The number of flowers on each spike is also variable – usually 2–8 but sometimes more. Plants will remain in flower for up to five weeks.

Temperature

- At night: 13–15°C (55–59°F)
- During the day: 18–24°C (64–75°F)

Position

- Good, but diffused, light suits a Miltonia best. When the plant is positioned further into a room, diffused light is not so important. Nevertheless, ensure that the leaves and flowers cannot be scorched by strong sunlight.

Watering

- The frequency of watering is influenced by the time of year and where the plant is positioned. Keep the compost evenly moist, although if a compost mixture of peat and perlite is used it is possible to let the compost become relatively dry before adding water. However, if peat becomes very dry it is difficult to encourage it to become moist. Additionally, remember that although the surface may appear dry the base may still be wet.

Humidity

- High humidity is essential around the plant. Therefore, you should stand the pot on moist gravel, taking care that the base of the pot is above the water level in the gravel.

Feeding

- Add a specific orchid fertilizer to the watering water. However, omit the fertilizer at every third or fourth watering.
- Always use a proprietary orchid fertilizer and do not exceed the manufacturer's recommended concentration or frequency rate. When used excessively and in strong concentrations, fertilizers can damage the roots of an orchid.
- If your Miltonia is not in good condition and growing strongly, do not feed it until the roots are better developed.

Repotting and compost

- Repot your Miltonia every other year, sometime between late winter and mid-spring for young plants that are not at their flowering stage. For flowering plants, repot in early autumn. Use a compost formed of two parts fibrous peat (with a pH of 6.2) and one part coarse perlite. It is also possible to add bark to the mixture.
- See page 37 for other suitable compost mixtures.

After flowering

- When flowering is complete, cut the flowering stem to 2.5–5 cm (1–2 in) of its base.

Checking for root development

An orchid pot eventually becomes congested with roots and repotting is advisable. Transparent pots readily enable the development of roots to be monitored.

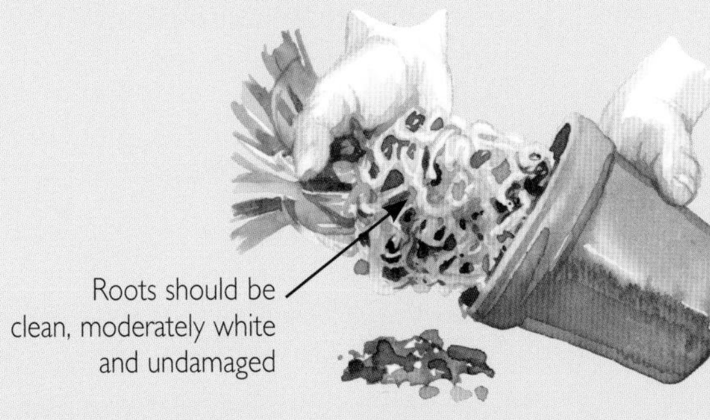

Roots should be clean, moderately white and undamaged

AFTER FLOWERING

When flowering is over, with many orchids it is advisable to cut down the stem which displayed flowers. Make a clean cut near to the base of the flowered stem.

Use sharp scissors or secateurs, cutting near the stem's base

A GUIDE TO GROWING ODONTOGLOSSUMS

Odontoglossum *Geyser Gold bears white flowers dappled with yellow.*

These distinctive epiphytic orchids have a wide range of colours and shapes, with the bonus of long-lasting flowers. Most Odontoglossums grown today are hybrids, with many being derived from *Odontoglossum crispum* which reveals frilled edges to its petals. Most plants produce only one flowering spike, although large plants occasionally have several. Flowering occurs from late autumn to late spring, with the flowers lasting 5–7 weeks.

Use a small saucer to catch any water that drains through the compost.

Temperature

- At night: 10–15°C (50–59°F)
- During the day: 15–23°C (59–73°F)

Warning: Do not give high temperatures when plants are in flower, as this shortens the life of the flowers. Rather, they enjoy a cool position.

Position

- Diffused, indirect light is best. Do not expose plants, especially when in flower, to strong and direct sunlight.

Watering

- The frequency of watering is influenced by the time of year and where the plant is positioned. You should keep the compost evenly moist but not waterlogged, and remember that although the surface may appear dry the base could be moist.
- The type of compost influences the frequency of watering; if the plant is grown in peat and perlite it can be allowed to dry out slightly between waterings. However, dry peat is very difficult to remoisten.
- Plants grown in sphagnum moss can be allowed to dry out slightly between waterings. If possible, use rainwater, especially when your plant is growing in sphagnum moss.

Humidity

- Your Odontoglossum delights in a moist atmosphere around its leaves and flowers. Therefore, stand the pot on moist gravel in a tray, but ensure that the base of the pot is not continually wet.

Feeding

- Add a specific orchid fertilizer to the watering water. However, remember to omit the fertilizer at every third or fourth watering.
- Always use a proprietary orchid fertilizer and do not exceed the manufacturer's recommended concentration or frequency rate. When used excessively and in strong concentrations, fertilizers can damage the roots of an orchid.
- If your Odontoglossum is not in good condition and growing strongly, do not feed it until the roots are better developed.

Repotting and compost

- Repot your Odontoglossum every other year, sometime between late winter and mid-spring for young plants that are not at their flowering stage. For flowering plants, repot in early autumn.
- Use a compost formed of two parts fibrous peat (with a pH of 6.2) and one part coarse perlite. It is also possible to add bark to the mixture. Alternatively, use a mixture of sphagnum moss and perlite.
- See page 37 for other suitable compost mixtures.

After flowers fade, use sharp scissors or secateurs to cut near the stem's base.

After flowering

- When flowering is complete, cut the flower stem to about 2.5 cm (1 in) of its base.

SUPPORTING FLOWER STEMS

Most orchids are borne on stems that are self-supporting. Others have pendulous stems, while some develop main stems that need to be secured with soft string to a thin cane, perhaps every few centimetres along its length. In addition, other orchids (such as Cattleyas) have large flowers that need individual support: secure the main flowering stem to a split bamboo cane and, in a 'maypole' arrangement, individually support the flower stems.

A GUIDE TO GROWING PAPHIOPEDILUMS

➚ Paphiopedilum sukhakulii, *native to Thailand, is a popular Slipper Orchid, with attractively coloured petals and lip.*

These superb orchids are widely known as Slipper Orchids, because of the lip-shaped pouch at the front of the flower. The flowers are usually long-lasting and often remain in bloom for around three months. Most hybrids produce only a single flower, but 'multiflorals' will have several on each stem.

Temperature

Those with mottled leaves:
- At night: 18°C (64°F)
- During the day: 21°C (70°F)

Those with plain green leaves:
- At night: 13°C (55°F)
- During the day: 18°C (64°F)

Position

- Good but indirect light is best. Do not expose plants to direct and strong sunlight.

Watering

- The frequency of watering is influenced by the time of year and where the plant is positioned. You should keep the compost evenly moist but not waterlogged, and remember that, although the surface may appear dry, the base could be moist.
- The type of compost influences the frequency of watering. If your plant is grown in peat and perlite, allow it to dry out slightly between waterings – but remember that dry peat is very difficult to remoisten.
- Plants grown in sphagnum moss should not be allowed to dry out between waterings. If possible, use rainwater, especially when your plant is growing in sphagnum moss.

Humidity

- Your Paphiopedilum needs a moist atmosphere around its leaves and flowers. Therefore, stand the pot on moist gravel in a tray. However, you should ensure that the base of the pot is not continually wet.

Feeding

- Add a specific orchid fertilizer to the watering water. However, remember to omit the fertilizer at every third or fourth watering.
- Always use a proprietary orchid fertilizer and do not exceed the manufacturer's recommended concentration or frequency rate. When they are used excessively and in strong concentrations, fertilizers can damage the roots of an orchid.
- If your Paphiopedilum is not in good condition and growing strongly, do not feed it until the roots are better developed. Do not exceed the manufacturer's recommended concentration as the roots may then be damaged.

Repotting and compost

- Repot your plant in early or mid-spring. Use a well-aerated and freely draining compost such as two parts fibrous peat (with a pH of 6.2) and one part coarse perlite. Sometimes, bark is added to this mixture. Alternatively, use a compost formed of three parts sphagnum moss and one part coarse perlite.
- See page 37 for other suitable compost mixtures.

After flowering

- When flowering is over, use sharp scissors or secateurs to cut down the flower stem to about 2.5 cm (1 in) above its base.

➚ Paphiopedilum *Maudiae 'Alba' has a distinctive shape, especially seen from the front.*

CLEANING LEAVES

Water stains and dust on leaves are unsightly, but can be easily removed. While a leaf is being cleaned, hold its base to prevent it being pulled out. Young leaves on Odontoglossums and Cymbidiums are especially vulnerable to being tugged off. While holding the leaf's base, draw a damp sponge upwards along it. Additionally, at this time, take the opportunity to wipe the pot clean.

Dirty leaves are a symptom of neglect. Regularly clean the leaves, but take care not to pull them off.

A GUIDE TO GROWING PHALAENOPSIS

Phalaenopisis *Dragon's Charm has speckling on a light yellow background.*

Often known as Moth Orchids, these epiphytic orchids are widely grown and well suited to life indoors. The flowers are long-lasting, often for up to three months.

Temperature

- At night: 16–18°C (61–64°F)
- During the day: 18–30°C (64–86°F)

Warning: Do not reduce the night temperature below 12°C (54°F) because then your plant will not develop flower buds.

Position

- Indirect light is essential for these orchids, especially at the height of summer. Net curtains are ideal for diffusing strong sunlight.

Watering

- The frequency of watering is influenced by the time of year and the position of your plant. You should keep the compost evenly moist but not waterlogged, and remember that, although the surface may appear dry, the base could be moist.
- The type of compost also influences the frequency of watering. If your plant is in a peat and perlite mixture it is essential to let the compost dry out slightly between waterings. However, remember that peat when dry is difficult to remoisten. Preferably, use a watering mixture of equal parts clean rainwater and tap water.
- If sphagnum moss is used as a compost, do not allow the compost to become dry between waterings and, if possible, use rainwater.

Humidity

- Your Phalaenopsis needs a moist atmosphere around its leaves and flowers. Therefore, stand the pot on moist gravel in a tray. However, you should make sure that the base of the pot is not continually wet. Additionally, mist-spray plants if the air is dry; this is best done in the morning so that all moisture on the leaves has evaporated by nightfall.

Phalaenopsis enjoy a humid atmosphere. Always mist-spray plants in the morning.

Feeding

- Add a specific orchid fertilizer to the watering water. However, remember to omit the fertilizer at every third or fourth watering.
- Always use a proprietary orchid fertilizer and do not exceed the manufacturer's recommended concentration or frequency rate. When used excessively and in strong concentrations, fertilizers can damage the roots of an orchid.

Repotting and compost

- Repot your orchid every other year between early spring and early summer. Use a well-aerated and free-draining compost such as two parts fibrous peat (with a pH of 6.2), one part coarse perlite and one part bark. Also, add a small amount of charcoal. Alternatively, use a compost formed of bark and chopped sphagnum moss.
- See page 37 for other suitable compost mixtures.

Flowering

- After the flowers fade, use sharp scissors or secateurs to cut the flowered stem back to just above a joint, leaving a stem about 30 cm (12 in) long. Further flowers may then be produced within 2–3 months. Plants do not have a yearly cycle of producing flowers and may develop flower spikes at any time of the year. However, should flowers not appear, reduce the temperature by 5°C (8°F) for four weeks.

ORCHIDS OUTDOORS

In temperate countries, some orchids, such as Cymbidiums, can be placed outdoors during summer. As well as giving them a holiday, they can create attractive features on patios or suspended in baskets from trees. They need regular attention, and watering and feeding are main considerations. Also, shading from bright sunlight is important to prevent leaves being damaged. Check that slugs and snails are unable to reach plants – stand them on low, wire-netting staging to prevent the intrusion of these pests, which appear at night and during warm, humid periods.

Cymbidiums create extra interest on patios during warm summers. Choose a wind-sheltered position.

A GUIDE TO GROWING ZYGOPETALUMS

These are distinctive epiphytic orchids, which are usually grown in a greenhouse. However, small types are ideal for placing on a windowsill where the light is diffused through net curtains. Many flowers are scented and in colours including purple, violet, brown, green, red and yellow. They flower mainly in spring and early summer and each plant develops several flower spikes.

Temperature

During winter
Day: 7–24°C (45–75°F)
Night: A significant drop in temperature at night is essential, but not below 7°C (45°F)

During summer
Day: 18–35°C (64–95°F)
Night: A significant drop in temperature at night is essential, but not below 13°C (55°F)

Standing a pot on a bed of glass balls creates extra interest and reflects light.

Position

- Diffused light is essential, although it should not be dark.

Watering

- The frequency of watering is influenced by the time of year and the plant's position. Keep the compost evenly moist but not waterlogged, and remember that, although the surface may appear dry, the base could be moist. Preferably, use a watering mixture of equal parts of clean rainwater and tap water.
- The type of compost influences the frequency of watering. If your plant is in a peat and perlite mixture, do not allow it to dry out between waterings because peat, when dry, is very difficult to remoisten.

Standing a pot on gravel creates humidity.

- If using a sphagnum moss compost, do not allow it to become dry between waterings and, if possible, use rainwater.

Humidity

- To ensure good humidity, stand the pot on moist gravel, but make sure the base is not constantly soaked.

Feeding

- Add a specific orchid fertilizer to the watering water, but omit the fertilizer at every third or fourth watering.
- Always use a proprietary orchid fertilizer and do not exceed the manufacturer's recommended concentration or frequency rate. When used excessively and in strong concentrations, fertilizers can damage the roots of an orchid.

Zygopetalum *Artur Elle 'Stonehouse' has distinctively shaped flowers.*

Repotting and compost

- Repot your orchid in spring or early summer. Take care not to move your plant into too large a pot – there should be only just enough room for the plant to develop two new pseudobulbs.
- Free-draining and well-aerated compost is essential. Therefore, use a mixture of two parts fibrous peat (with a pH of 6.2) and one part coarse perlite. Another good compost mixture is three parts sphagnum moss, one of coarse perlite, and one of bark.
- See page 37 for other suitable compost mixtures.

After flowering

- When the flowers fade, cut down the flower stem to about 2.5 cm (1 in) above the base.
- Healthy plants that are reluctant to bloom can be encouraged to develop flowers by placing them in a cool position for a few weeks.

RELUCTANCE TO PRODUCE FLOWERS

Occasionally, a healthy and well-established orchid fails to produce flowers. Invariably, this is because the light and temperature do not suit it. Check that it is being given the light intensity it needs at that time of the year, and that the temperature is suitable. Sometimes, orchids that are in a mixed group of plants will not readily flower because the conditions given to them suit the majority of plants, but not them. Try moving the plant to a warmer or cooler part of the greenhouse. However, avoid giving a shock to the plant by radically lowering the temperature as this may deter flowering for a complete season – or more. Also check that pests and diseases are not present (see pages 42–45).

Growing other indoor orchids

Can I grow other orchids indoors?

In addition to the detailed information about looking after Cymbidiums, Miltonias, Odontoglossums, Paphiopedilums, Phalaenopsis and Zygopetalums (pages 20–25), below there is some general information about other superb orchids that can be grown indoors. Specific clues to their success indoors and where they are best grown are given in the A–Z of orchids (pages 46–77). Many of these orchids are also suitable for conservatories (see below).

OTHER ORCHIDS TO CONSIDER

Listed below are ten other groups of orchids for you to consider growing. Note that only certain species and hybrids within the groups are suitable for growing indoors; examples of some of them are illustrated on the opposite page.

- **Cattleyas** (see page 49)
  This group includes related genera, of which there are many. Their relationship with Cattleyas is indicated in parts of their names; full details of the coding used by orchid nurseries and in books are provided on page 46.
- **Coelogynes** (see page 53)
- **Dendrobiums** (see page 58)
- **Laelias** (see page 62)
- **Lycastes** (see page 63)
- **Oncidiums** (see page 68)
- **Pleiones** (see page 74)
- **Stanhopeas** (see page 74)
- **Vandas** (see page 75)
- x **Vuylstekearas** (see page 76)

Conservatories and sunrooms
All of the orchids that are suggested on this and pages 20–25 are suitable for growing in conservatories and sunrooms, especially some of the larger-flowered types such as Cattleyas and related genera.

Positions

- Avoid positions where plants can be knocked, such as by heavy curtains during winter, by young children or by animals.
- Good but filtered light is essential and near an east- or west-facing window is ideal. Avoid positions in direct, strong sunlight.
- Avoid positions in draughts, whether cold or warm. Plants become chilled or overheated and both flowers and plants suffer. Also, for some orchids high temperatures can deter flowering.
- Special growing-cases create ideal places for cultivating some orchids (see page 18).

Temperatures

- Ideal temperatures vary from one species to another and these are indicated on pages 46–77. However, general daytime temperatures in summer of about 21°C (70°F) and 15°C (59°F) in winter are about right.
- Additionally, there should be a temperature fall at night to ensure that plants are not too active during the hours of darkness.

Humidity, watering and feeding

- Humidity is essential and regularly misting leaves is important, especially in summer when temperatures are at their highest and air driest. Preferably, mist-spray plants in the morning, so that moisture has evaporated by evening when the temperature falls. Do not dampen the flowers.
- Regularly check the compost to ensure that it remains moist but not waterlogged. Indeed, some orchids are best left until the surface of the compost is dry before applying further water.
- Preferably, use soft water.
- Feed orchids using only special orchid fertilizers.

Repotting

- Only repot orchids when their growth starts to be harmed. This is usually every 2–3 years, although some when young need yearly repotting.
- It is inevitable that a few roots on some species force their way outside of a pot; orchids in baskets often have roots pushing out from their sides.
- Use special orchid composts (see page 37).

FOR SUCCESS INDOORS

➚ Coelogyne crista *is, perhaps, the most popular species of its genus. It never fails to attract attention.*

➚ *Hybrids with* Cattleya *in their parentage are popular; Lake Murray 'Mendenhall' is a* Brassolaeliocattleya, *with* Brassovola, Cattleya *and* Laelia *in its parentage.*

➔ Laelia tenebrosa, *sometimes sold as* Laelia grandis *var.* tenebrosa, *has beautiful, fragrant flowers.*

➚ Lycastes skinneri *creates a feast of distinctive rich colour in spring.*

➚ *Pleiones are distinctive and ideal for growing in cool rooms.*

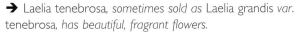

➚ x Vuylstekeara *Cambria 'Plush' is easy to grow in cool or warm rooms.*

Guide to greenhouse orchids

Are there orchids for greenhouses?

There is a wide range of orchids that can be grown in greenhouses (many are also candidates for growing indoors; see pages 20–27). In greenhouses, and to enable groups of orchids with similar temperature needs to be grown together, orchids can be arranged into three different temperature regimes. These are 'cool', 'intermediate' and 'warm'. The temperatures associated with each of these groups are indicated on the opposite page.

BALANCING TEMPERATURE, LIGHT AND HUMIDITY

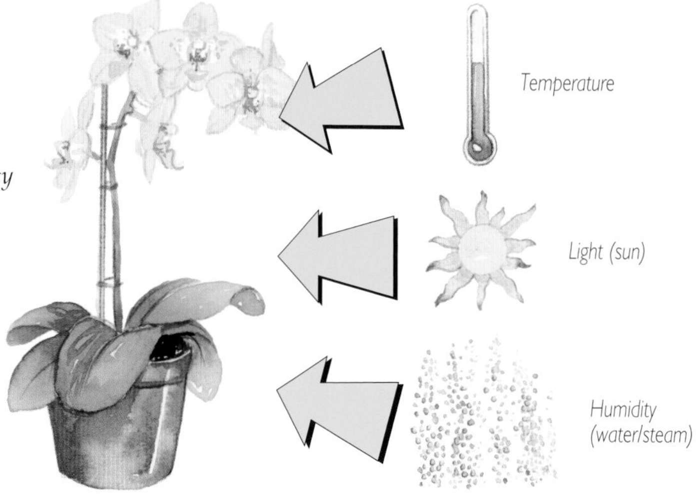

Temperature, light and humidity all influence the growth and well-being of orchids. They need to be 'in balance' with each other.

- **In the wild** there is a balance between light intensity and temperature.
- **When plants** are grown in an alien environment there are conflicting influences on the creation of an ideal environment. Either the temperature is too high and the light intensity too low, or the natural balance of humidity, temperature and light is upset. Therefore, growing orchids in greenhouses – as well as indoors – is always a compromise.
- **In nature,** a combination of high humidity and high temperature is not worrying, but in a greenhouse a late evening and night combination of a low temperature and high humidity can encourage the presence of diseases. For this reason, preferably mist-spray and water plants in the morning, so that excess water has evaporated by nightfall.

With orchids on benches as well as suspended, a greenhouse becomes awash with colour.

Is it expensive to heat a greenhouse?

The cost of heating a greenhouse rises dramatically for each increased degree of temperature. Part of this problem is the greater heat loss from a greenhouse that is kept at high temperatures. See pages 32–33 for heating and insulating a greenhouse.

GREENHOUSE TEMPERATURES FOR ORCHIDS

Orchids can be grouped according to their temperature requirements during summer and winter.

COOL		INTERMEDIATE		WARM	
Orchids need a minimum winter night temperature of 10°C (50°F), rising to a maximum summer day temperature of 24°C (75°F).	24°C 75°F ↕ 10°C 50°F	Orchids need a minimum winter night temperature of 13°C (55°F), rising to a maximum summer day temperature of 24°C (75°F).	24°C 75°F ↕ 13°C 55°F	Orchids need a minimum winter night temperature not less than 18°C (64°F), and preferably in the region of 21°C (70°F). During the day a rise of 5°C (10°F) is essential.	26°C 80°F ↕ 21°C 70°F

***Note:** throughout the A–Z of orchids (pages 46–77) the temperature required for each orchid is indicated.*

Instant guide to temperature requirements

The range of orchids for greenhouses is wide. To enable novice orchid enthusiasts to assess which are suitable for the temperatures in their greenhouse, the following groupings will be useful. However, remember that the temperature in a greenhouse will vary – the lower parts are usually cooler than positions towards the top of the structure. Tiered staging that utilizes different temperature regimes is featured on page 35, with display inspirations on page 34.

Before deciding on the types of orchids to buy, over a week check the temperatures in your greenhouse by using a 'minimum and maximum' thermometer (see below right). The orchids listed below are grouped into three temperature regimes and will give an indication of which orchids to buy (others are described on pages 46–77).

'Cool' orchids

- *Anguloa clowesii* (see page 47)
- *Bifrenaria harrisoniae* (see page 47)
- *Brassia verrucosa* (see page 48)
- *Bulbophyllum careyanum* (see page 48)
- *Cattleya aurantiaca* (see page 49)
- *Cirrhopetalum umbellatum* (see page 53)
- *Coelogyne cristata* (see page 53)
- *Cymbidium eburneum* (see page 54)
- *Cymbidium sanderae* (see page 54)
- *Dendrobium densiflorum* (see page 58)
- *Dendrobium farmeri* (see page 58)
- *Dendrobium nobile* (see page 59)
- *Encyclia cochleata* (see page 60)
- *Encyclia radiata* (see page 60)
- *Epidendrum parkinsonianum* (see page 61)
- *Gongora truncata* (see page 62)
- *Laelia anceps* (see page 62)
- *Masdevallia coccinea* (see page 63)
- *Maxillaria hematoglossa* (see page 64)
- *Maxillaria praestans* (see page 64)
- *Odontoglossum cariniferum* (see page 67)
- *Oncidium ornithorhynchum* (see page 68)
- *Pleione formosana* (see page 74)
- *Stanhopea eburnea* (see page 75)
- *Stanhopea platyceras* (see page 75)

'Intermediate' orchids

- *Aspasia lunata* (see page 47)
- *Cattleya bowringiana* (see page 49)
- *Dendrobium* Gatton Sunray (see page 58)
- *Encyclia brassavolae* (see page 60)
- *Epidendrum ciliare* (see page 61)
- *Epidendrum* Pink Cascade (see page 61)
- *Gongora quinquenervis* (see page 62)
- *Laelia pulcherrima* (see page 62)
- *Laelia purpurata* (see page 62)
- *Maxillaria camaridii* (see page 63)
- *Miltonia clowesii* (see page 64)
- *Miltonia spectabilis* (see page 64)
- *Oncidium ampliatum* (see page 68)
- *Oncidium macranthum* (see page 68)
- *Phragmipedium besseae* (see page 73)
- *Vanda coerulea* (see page 75)

'Warm' orchids

- *Angraecum sesquipedale* (see page 47)
- *Coelogyne asperata* (see page 53)
- *Paphiopedilum* Delophyllum (see page 69)
- *Phalaenopsis* Cool Breeze (see page 70)
- *Phalaenopsis* Flare Spots (see page 70)
- *Phragmipedium pearcei* (see page 73)
- *Vanda sanderana* (see page 76)

TEMPERATURE TRENDS

In earlier years, most orchids grown by orchid enthusiasts were given high temperatures, and this made growing orchids a hobby for wealthy people who could afford to heat specially constructed greenhouses to high temperatures throughout the year. Later, it was realized that many orchids would grow in much lower temperatures, while in recent years the trend has been to select those orchids that grow and flower indoors.

'Warmth-loving' orchids include:
- *Angraecum sesquipedale* (see page 47)
- *Coelogyne asperata* (see page 53)

Angraecum sesquipedale *is easy to grow and produces star-shaped flowers in winter.*

'Cool-growing' types for indoor cultivation include:
- *Coelogyne ochracea* (see page 54)
- *Dendrobium farmeri* (see page 58)
- *Encyclia radiata* (see page 60)

ASSESSING THE TEMPERATURE

Regularly check the temperature by using a 'minimum and maximum' thermometer. These useful instruments enable the temperature to be recorded from one day to another, as well as checking that the heating system is correctly achieving the desired temperature, both at night and during the daytime.

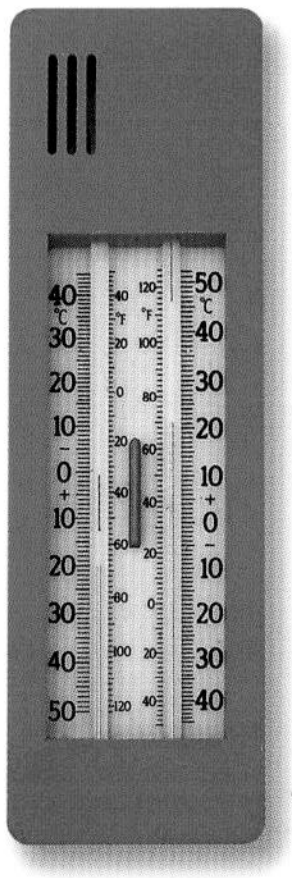

'Minimum and maximum' thermometers are essential for assessing temperatures through the day and night.

Greenhouses for growing orchids

What is the best size for a greenhouse?

An orchid greenhouse needs be at least 3.6 m by 2.4 m (12 ft by 8 ft), or 3 m (10 ft) square. Greenhouses that are smaller than this will not give you enough path and display space. In addition, small greenhouses become excessively hot in summer, while in the winter months the limited amount of air retains little residual warmth. Just as importantly, as your enthusiasm for orchids grows a large greenhouse becomes an essential feature.

Range of greenhouses

Often, a greenhouse is inherited with a new garden and can be one of several designs. Some greenhouses can be easily modified for growing orchids, while others present greater problems – some are impossible to overcome.

Types of greenhouse

Even-span greenhouses are popular and modern ones have glass from ground to ridge and with an aluminium framework. Earlier types were made of wood, with brick or wood sides to about 75 cm (30 in) high. There should be top and side ventilators.

Even-span

Octagonal greenhouses are modernistic and usually with limited ventilation. They are small and inadequately ventilated unless the door is left open. They allow abundant sun to enter, but with orchids this is a disadvantage.

Octagonal

Lean-to greenhouses are usually built against a house wall and with a sunny aspect. Modern types have an aluminium framework, but older ones are wood with brick or wooden sides to 75 cm (30 in) high. Ventilators in the roof and sides are essential.

Lean-to

Miniature lean-to greenhouses are popular for small summer displays and seed-raised plants in spring, but their limited air volume and inaccessibility – usually only 60 cm (2 ft) deep and about 1.5 m (5 ft) high – mean they are not suitable for orchids.

Miniature lean-to

Other greenhouses

Plastic tunnels formed of heavy-gauge polythene or PVC sheeting stretched over metal hoops about 1.8 m (6 ft) high are popular, but the life of the covering is limited, while ventilation, rapid heat loss and condensation are problems.

With a medley of orchids, a greenhouse becomes a colourful array of leaves and flowers throughout the year. Remember to grow some plants in baskets.

LOCATION AND ORIENTATION OF A GREENHOUSE

- **Location:** Orchid greenhouses are used throughout the year and therefore need to be near a house and joined by an all-weather path. Electricity and a water supply need to be installed.
- **Orientation:** Position even-span greenhouses with the ridge running east to west. This gives more winter sunshine than north–south orientation. Position the door away from cold and prevailing wind. Lean-to greenhouses need a sunny aspect.

GOOD AND BAD POSITIONS FOR GREENHOUSES

Avoid positions under large trees which lose their leaves in autumn.

Avoid winter shade from buildings or large evergreen hedges or trees.

In winter a coniferous hedge 3.6 ft (12 ft) away on the cold side reduces heat loss.

Position the greenhouse near to the top of a slope rather than at its base.

GREENHOUSE VENTILATION

Ventilation and shading are the main ways to prevent temperatures in an orchid house rising too high in summer, as well as stopping strong sunlight scorching leaves and flowers.

There are three main temperature regimes recommended for orchids in greenhouses, and these are detailed on pages 28–29. These vary between summer and winter, and from night to day.

Ideal ventilation and shading may be achieved during the day, but at night heating is usually needed (see pages 32–33), especially in winter.

Slatted roller-blinds

These prevent strong sunlight reaching the inside of a greenhouse. They are supported on metal runners and held clear of the glass to enable ventilators in the roof to open and close. Cords enable them to be run up and down, according to the strength of the sunlight.

Automatic window-openers

Essential for all greenhouses as they open and close ventilators whether you are there or not. They can be preset to operate at the desired temperature and are invaluable to greenhouse hobbyists who are away from home during the day.

Louvred windows

Ideal for fitting at shoulder height into the sides or ends of a greenhouse. They help to reduce high temperatures and can be angled to allow fresh air to enter without causing draughts. They can be used to replace panes in all-glass greenhouses.

Ventilation hole

Installed into brickwork or wood-based surrounds of greenhouse, ventilation holes enable fresh air to enter at near ground level and to pass out of ventilators at the top without creating unnecessary draughts. They can be used in conjunction with extractor fans in the roof.

ALTERNATIVE SHADING

- **Whitewash:** an inexpensive way to keep greenhouses cool in summer. Apply the whitewash layer in spring, but it may need renewing before its removal in late autumn.
- **Greenhouse netting:** secure this to the outside of a greenhouse to shade plants and reflect heat. During dull periods it can be removed, as well as during winter.

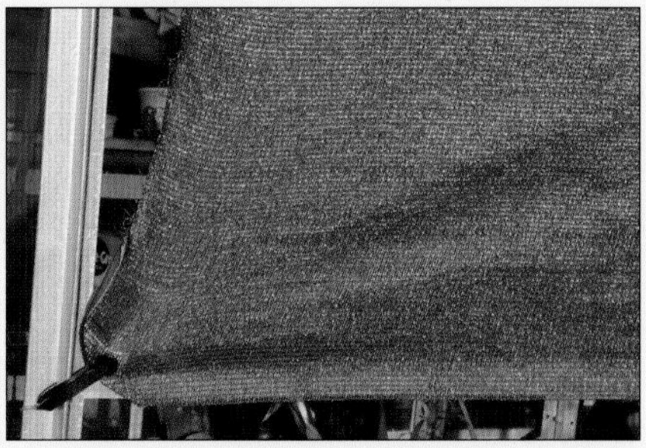

Ensure that the netting cannot be blown away.

TEMPERATURE LAYERS

Within the same greenhouse, differing temperature regimes can be achieved by positioning plants on staging at various heights. For example, at waist height the temperature is lower than in the roof area – but do not risk overheating plants and remember that excessive sun damages them. Use a 'minimum and maximum' thermometer to check temperatures at differing levels. Displaying orchids at different heights is detailed on pages 34–35.

Heating and cooling greenhouses

How do I get the right temperature?

Achieving the desired warmth in a greenhouse is always a balance between heating and cooling and because temperatures vary throughout the day it was earlier considered a skill only to be gained from experience. Today, there are many temperature-controlling devices that orchid growers can use to ensure the temperature is right. These vary from static thermostats to devices that draw in air from a wide area and then either cool or add warmth.

Electric, thermostatically controlled heaters are efficient and easy to operate; ensure that cables and plugs are waterproof.

HEATING AND COOLING

- **Heat** in small, modern greenhouses is provided through paraffin heaters or electrical heating controlled by a thermostat. Paraffin heaters create warmth and give off moisture, which needs to escape through a ventilator. They are efficient, but if badly maintained and with a wick too high will produce smoke. Electrical heaters are cleaner and more efficient; however, they must always be installed by a competent electrician.
- **Cooling** is invariably achieved by opening ventilators (see page 31) or electrical extractor fans linked to a thermostat.

Temperature is critical

Providing the correct temperature for orchids is vital for their welfare. It is also essential as a way to save money – heating costs rise dramatically with each increased degree in warmth.

Ventilation and shading

Ventilation can be provided by automatic ventilators (see page 31). Shading, however, is not readily automated; whitewash and gauze-netting will need to be removed manually.

SYMPTOMS IF TOO HOT

- **The atmosphere** will become increasingly dry as the temperature rises. This causes the edges of leaves and flowers to dry and, eventually, become crisp and brown. More frequent damping down and syringing will be essential to keep the atmosphere humid.
- **Compost** will dry rapidly and plants will need more frequent watering.
- **'Cool'-temperature** orchids will rapidly become exhausted and, eventually, wilt.
- **Pests** will become more prevalent. Check for webbing on plants and spray as necessary. Syringing with clean water is a deterrent.

HEATING GREENHOUSES

Paraffin heater

Paraffin heaters are available in several sizes and are inexpensive to buy and operate. They are versatile and can be easily moved from one greenhouse to another. With this type of heater, oxygen is consumed and carbon dioxide given off. Therefore, it is essential to open a ventilator (or operate an extractor fan) to remove fumes. Additionally, they create moisture; it has been estimated that when paraffin is burnt an equal volume of water vapour is produced.

Always check a paraffin heater each evening to ensure the wick is not excessively long, and the fuel tank is full so that it will not run dry during the night.

Some electric fan-heaters have built-in thermostats. Plug into a waterproof socket and place on the floor of a greenhouse, with the warm air passing down the path area and not directly on plants. Take care not to splash water on a fan-heater when mist-spraying or watering.

Other electrical heaters include tubular heaters which are secured to the inside of a greenhouse wall and operated by a thermostat. Ensure that hot air can rise freely.

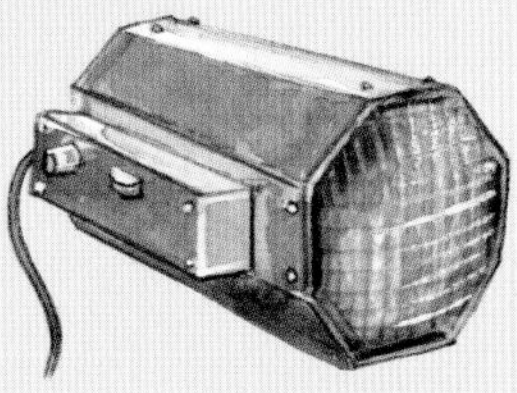

Electric fan-heater

SYMPTOMS IF TOO COLD

- **The atmosphere** will become increasingly damp as the temperature falls and may cause dampness to remain too long around the plants, especially at night. This may encourage mould to appear on the pots and plants.
- **Moisture** will remain longer on the floor and around plants.
- **Composts** will not require such frequent watering.
- **'Warm'-temperature** orchids will suffer first, with lack of growth and a general malaise.
- **Pests such as slugs and snails** will become bolder and venture out more – use baits, as necessary.

COOLING GREENHOUSES

Cooling the air in a greenhouse in summer is just as important as heating the area in winter. Temperatures can rise dramatically, even on a clouded summer's day.

Circulating fans
These are not fans that extract hot air from a greenhouse but move air around, perhaps drawing in both hot and cool air and merging them. Additionally, they create a buoyant atmosphere, preventing a build-up of damp air which could encourage diseases.

Electric circulating fan

Extractor fans
These are usually fitted into a gable end (usually the one opposite the door) of a greenhouse and are ideal for rapidly reducing the temperature. They are controlled by a thermostat and can be adjusted to operate at specific temperatures.

Electric extractor fan

ORCHIDS IN CONSERVATORIES

Sometimes, domestic hot-water radiator systems are extended into conservatories and, at first thought, may appear to be ideal places for orchids. However, as domestic heating systems are usually turned down at night – when plants are most vulnerable from low temperatures – this is not practical unless an electrical fan-heater is also present.

INSULATING GREENHOUSES

As a way to cut winter heating costs, try insulating your greenhouse. This can be achieved by securing **plastic bubble-wrap insulation** to the inside of your greenhouse. This type of insulation material is formed of three layers of plastic sheeting with bubbles of air between them. Secure it in place with double-sided adhesive pads, drawing pins or thumb tacks in wooden greenhouses, and special clips in aluminium greenhouses. Check that the ventilators can still be opened.

Troubleshooting

PROBLEM	SOLUTION
Heating system fails – plants appear sick, especially those growing at the top of the greenhouse and near the glass.	If electrical: check fuse boxes in case there is a short and they have tripped out. If cause is not readily apparent, call in an electrician. If paraffin-fuelled: check that the wick is not burned out or that the tank is not empty. Rectify as applicable.
Draughts – plants growing near doors and ventilators wilt and become sick and unsightly.	Fit draught-excluders around doors and ventilators. Also check that panes of glass are not cracked or broken. Keep a piece of polythene as a first-aid repair for a broken pane; use sticky tape to hold it in place before a proper repair can be made.
Excessive heating costs – fuel bills are high.	Check for draughts (see above) and plant an evergreen coniferous hedge on the cold side of the greenhouse. This will reduce the wind's speed and its ability to cool a greenhouse in winter. Plant the hedge about 3.6 m (12 ft) away from the greenhouse.

USING A GREENHOUSE THERMOMETER

The best thermometer in a greenhouse is a 'minimum and maximum' type (see page 29), which is ideal for monitoring temperatures over a 24-hour period or less. Read the temperatures each morning and reset the indicators, usually by pressing a button or using a special magnet. It is a good way of checking that the heating system is achieving the desired night temperature.

USING AN AUTOMATIC TEMPERATURE-CONTROL DEVICE

This device should be positioned at about shoulder height in a greenhouse and about two-thirds along its length. It works by continually drawing in air and passing it over a sensitive thermostat which controls both the heating and ventilation within the greenhouse. Ensure that the device is not positioned near to a door or a ventilator, as this influences its ability accurately to detect the general temperature. Ensure that a properly installed power supply is available.

Displaying orchids in greenhouses

How should I display greenhouse orchids?

There are several ways to display orchids, and the type of greenhouse you have influences the possible methods. Shelving can be constructed against a wall in lean-to greenhouses, while in traditional orchid houses tiered staging on one side and benching at waist height on the other are possibilities. In a modern equal-span greenhouse, benching at waist height is normal. Orchids grown in baskets or on pieces of bark can be suspended from walls or hooks in the roof.

Most greenhouse orchids are grown in pots and displayed on staging.

Some orchids, such as Stanhopeas, are best grown in slatted baskets.

Orchids with tall stems can be given decorative and artistic backgrounds.

WAYS OF DISPLAYING ORCHIDS IN A GREENHOUSE

- **On benches at waist height:** this is a popular way, especially in modern greenhouses with limited height. Position shade-loving orchids on the shadiest side of the greenhouse, and those that need more light on the brightest.
- **On tiered staging:** this can be constructed in high-roofed traditional orchid houses. It enables cool-loving plants to be placed low down, and warmth-loving ones higher up. It also allows plants with arching stems to be placed high up.
- **On shelves:** these are ideal for securing to brick or wood walls in lean-to greenhouses. Position narrow shelves towards the top, with wider ones below.
- **In baskets:** suspend these from hooks secured in the roof. Check that the basket will not be knocked, and water will not drip on other plants.
- **On pieces of bark, tree-fern fibre or cork bark:** either secure them to walls (ideal in lean-to greenhouses) or suspend from the roof. Again, ensure water will not drip on other plants. Additionally, they can be fixed to large-mesh green plastic netting draped from the roof.

ACCESSIBLE PLANTS

Always ensure that the plants in your greenhouse can be easily reached for watering and feeding as well as for checking that they are free from pests and diseases.

Display inspirations

Orchid houses become homes to a wide range of orchids that create magnificent displays throughout the year, but often at different times. Some orchids are best left in a greenhouse throughout their lives, while others can be taken indoors when in flower. Growing and displaying orchids indoors is described on pages 14–15, but here we suggest ways to get the best display in your greenhouse.

Orchid houses need to be more than a collection of plants growing in pots. Orchids are beautiful and adaptable plants and are ideal for creating special displays:

- A 1.5 m (5 ft) long tree trunk – about 15 m (6 in) wide and inserted about 30 cm (12 in) into the ground – can be covered with bark-loving orchids.
- A basket with trailing stems as a centrepiece and orchids growing on pieces bark, tree-fern fibre or cork bark suspended around it.
- Orchids like high humidity, so position a miniature water garden in a half-tub in one corner of the greenhouse. Add a miniature waterlily to the display.
- Many orchids have superb fragrance and introduce an inspirational quality to orchid houses.
- Install a few battery-powered display spotlights so that groups of orchids can be admired.

Use 'cool' lights to enhance plants.

DESIGN AND LAYOUT

Orchids have been grown in greenhouses for many decades, and therefore it is not surprising that there are several different designs and materials used in their construction. Additionally, there is a range of surfaces to choose from, and various ways to display plants.

Galvanized mesh benching

➔ Relatively modern design, formed of rust-resistant mesh secured to a wood or metal framework and tailored to a greenhouse's shape and size. It enables air to circulate around plants.

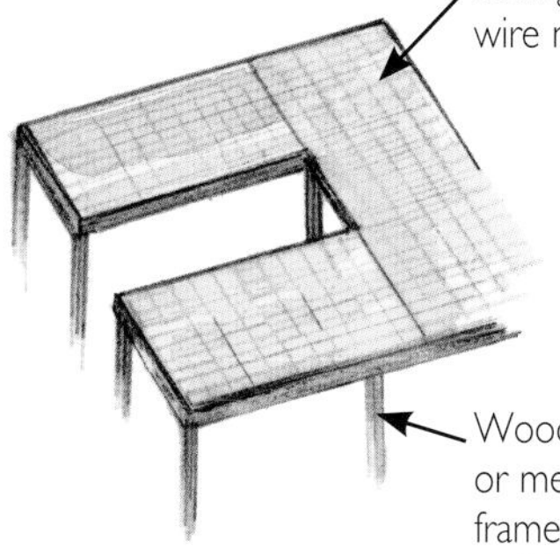

Modern equal-span greenhouse

➘ In wide greenhouses, two paths are needed to ensure plants can be reached. Slatted wood or galvanized mesh staging is ideal for supporting plants.

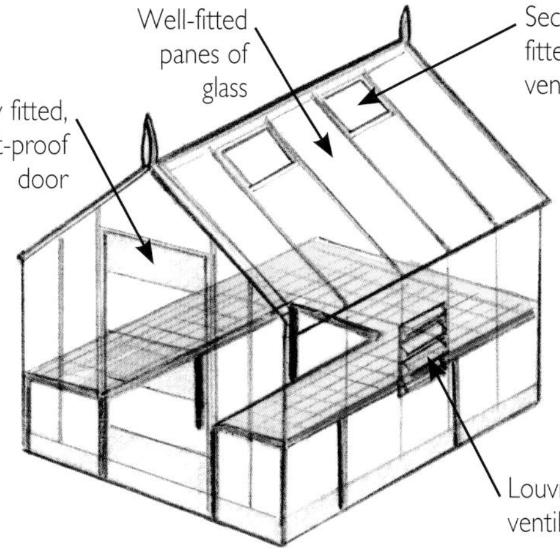

Tiered staging in a traditional orchid greenhouse

➘ Some orchid houses are tall or have offset spans. The highest part is ideal for housing tiered staging and this is constructed either totally of wood or of a metal framework supporting slatted wood or wire-mesh surfaces for display.

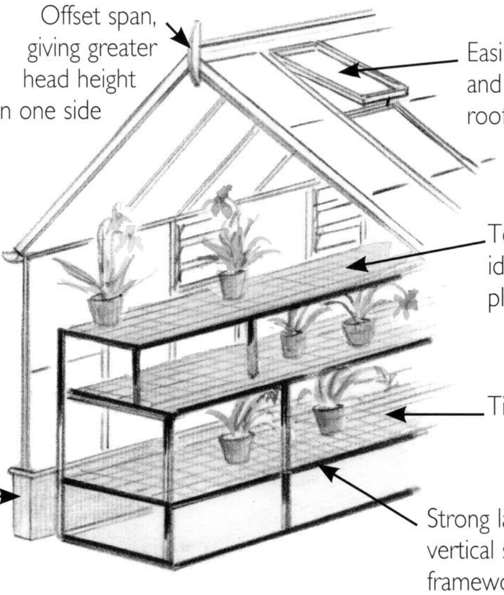

Shelves in lean-to greenhouses

➘ When fixing shelving to walls, ensure that they are well secured. Preferably, construct a metal frame which can be fixed to a wall, with shelving added.

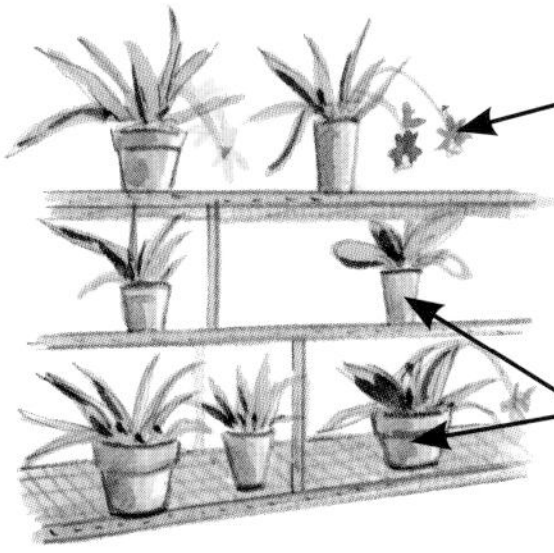

SECTIONING OFF A GREENHOUSE

Few gardeners have more than one greenhouse and this invariably has to accommodate orchids with different temperature needs. In summer, this is usually easy to achieve, but in winter it can be difficult (and expensive) to create high temperatures throughout a large greenhouse. However, by using a sheet of polythene to section off a greenhouse, the area to be heated is decreased and the problem made easier. However, ensure that there is adequate ventilation and that easy access will be possible at all times.

Grouping and sectioning off orchids with similar temperature requirements reduces heating costs, especially in winter.

FRAGRANT CORNERS

Several orchids are superbly scented and will enrich your life. There are many to choose from, and several are described in the A–Z of orchids (see pages 46–77). Here, however, are a few especially to consider:

- *Anguloa clowesii* – see page 47
- *Brassia verrucosa* – see page 48
- *Cattleya* – see page 49
- *Coelogyne ochracea* – see page 54
- *Dendrochilum cobbianum* – see page 59
- *Encyclia radiata* – see page 60
- *Gongora galeata* – see page 61
- *Oncidium ornithorhynchum* – see page 68

Remember to position them away from doors; otherwise their fragrance will be quickly dispersed.

Watering, misting, composts and feeding

Is watering orchids a problem?

Watering orchids is not difficult, but the frequency varies from one orchid to another – depending on its type and size – as well as the time of year and the type of compost in which it is growing. Some composts are more free-draining than others. Additionally, the technique of applying water to orchids differs depending on whether they are growing in pots, in baskets or are secured to bark. Orchids also need misting and feeding to keep them growing well.

ALL-EMBRACING HOBBY

Growing orchids is a hobby that demands attention every day and throughout the year. If possible, orchids need to be inspected several times a day, but in a realistic world this is not always possible. Automatic ventilation and heating are possible, and these are described on pages 32–33. Automatic watering is impractical in a small greenhouse where the range of orchids is wide, however. Apart from watering and feeding orchids, misting and damping down are essential to create a humid atmosphere. In a greenhouse, mist-spray water under benches and around pots. This may need to be done several times during a hot day, but ensure that all moisture has evaporated and leaf surfaces are dry by evening when the temperature naturally falls. Moist surfaces at night encourage the presence of diseases.

WATERING TECHNIQUES

'Over the rim'

↓ Watering 'over the rim' from the spout of a watering-can is the best way to water orchids growing in pots. Gently pour water into the gap between the compost and the pot's rim, so that the compost becomes thoroughly wet. Allow excess water to drain freely. Try to keep the water off the leaves. Some orchids, such as Cymbidiums and those congested with roots, force the rootball upwards and make watering difficult. At that stage, repotting is essential (see page 38).

Neglected roots

↙ If the roots of plants become exceptionally dry – perhaps after a long resting period or following neglect – immerse the rootball, still in its pot, in a bucket or bowl of clean water. When bubbles cease to rise, remove the plant and allow any excess water to drain away.

Grown on bark or other base

→ Plants growing on a piece of attractive bark or other base need to be taken down and dipped in water about once a week. With roots that are exposed and with little compost, they rapidly become dry. Daily – or more frequent – misting helps to keep compost and roots moist.

MISTING ORCHIDS

Orchids in baskets

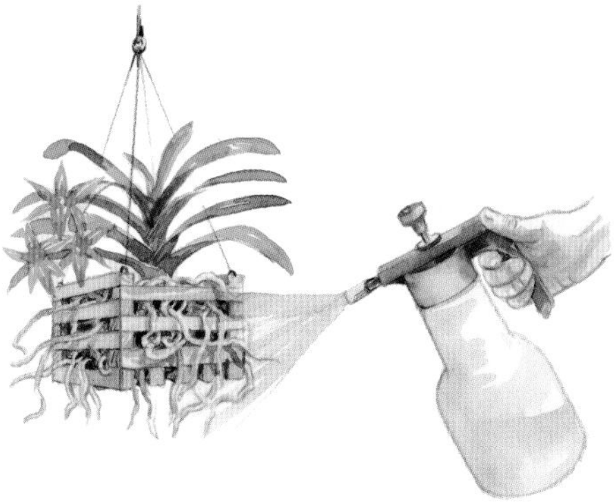

↗ Orchids growing in baskets need frequent misting to keep roots moist and active. Orchids tend to fill a basket with roots, which then spread outside of it and in a dry atmosphere soon become inactive.

Orchids on bark or other base

↗ Orchids growing on bark or other attractive base which is suspended or positioned against a wall or plastic mesh need regular and frequent misting.

Misting under benches

↗ Regularly misting under benches, as well as around pots, helps to increase humidity around plants. This technique is essential in greenhouses when the temperature is high.

COMPOSTS FOR ORCHIDS

Composts recommended for orchids vary from one expert to another, as well as between the orchids that suit them. On pages 20–25, compost mixtures to suit popular groups of orchids – Cymbidiums, Odontoglossums, Miltonias, Paphiopedilums, Phalaenopsis and Zygopetalums – are suggested. Alternative compost mixtures include:

- bark-based compost;
- three parts sphagnum moss, one part coarse perlite and one of bark;
- equal parts rockwool (absorbent type) and polyurethane foam;
- sphagnum moss and perlite;
- chopped coconut husk.

The range is wide and can appear bewildering to hobbyists new to growing orchids, but it need not be. Essentially, when buying an orchid ask about the compost, and when repotting use the same mixture. These can usually be bought ready for use from orchid nurseries.

After a few years, you may wish to experiment with other mixtures, but remember that the frequency of watering is influenced by the nature of the compost. Additionally, always ensure that the compost is clean and cannot become contaminated with pests while being stored.

WHAT IS pH?

It is represented on a scale that shows the degree of alkalinity or acidity in compost. The scale ranges from 1 to 14: pH 7.0 is neutral, figures below that indicate increasing acidity and those above increasing alkalinity (chalkiness).

It is possible to influence the pH of compost by adding ground limestone. The assessment of pH in compost (or in garden soil) can be done by using a pH chemical testing outfit. Alternatively, some pH testers need only a probe to be inserted into the compost and this is ideal for gardeners who are red/green colour blind. With the chemical method an assessment of colour is needed to indicate the pH.

Orchids require slightly acid compost – pH from 6.0 to 6.5, but usually 6.2.

FEEDING ORCHIDS

Earlier there was a myth that orchids did not need to be fed because they grew on trees and were not linked to the ground. Erroneously, they were thought to live solely on fresh air! Clearly this was wrong. Here are a few clues to successful feeding.

- Only feed orchids when they are in active growth.
- Feed orchids by adding plant foods to water when watering them.
- Buy reputable brands of plant food and adhere to their instructions.
- Too strong mixtures of plant food will damage the roots of orchids.
- Do not excessively feed orchids. Recommendations range from feeding orchids at each watering, but missing out on every third or fourth application, to feeding only on every second or third watering.

Watering tips

Knowing when and how much water to give a plant is a skill usually acquired through experience, but with orchids there are some clues to success.

- Water orchids during their periods of active growth.
- During resting periods some orchids can be left unwatered, while others need to have the compost kept slightly damp. For specific tips on watering popular groups of orchids, see pages 20–27. Clues to success with others are given in the A–Z of orchids (pages 46–77).

Repotting an orchid

When should I repot my orchid?

In general, orchids need repotting when their roots fill the pot and there is no further room for the development of pseudobulbs, if present. This is usually every 2–3 years, although some orchids – such as Cymbidiums and those growing strongly – are repotted more often. Repot in spring, but not if the orchid is in flower. In orchid terminology, repotting is sometimes known as 'dropping on', and you may see this term in books, as well as mentioned by orchid enthusiasts.

Do all orchids need repotting?

At some stage all orchids need repotting to provide them with fresh compost and space for roots to grow. Avoid repotting orchids into pots that are too large.

HEALTH-CHECK TIME

When repotting an orchid, check the plant's health. Cut off any dead, old and leafless pseudobulbs and dead roots. Also cleanly cut off damaged or dead leaves and check that soil pests are not present (see pages 42–43 for pests that can be found in compost).

SUITABLE POTS

Traditionally, clay pots were used when repotting orchids, because moisture could evaporate through them and keep the compost and roots cool. Nowadays, plastic pots are popular as they are lighter and cheaper. They keep the compost damp because moisture cannot pass through them.

Pots in natural colours are popular, but increasingly opaque ones are favoured by nurseries as they enable roots to remain active for longer than when in pots with a solid colour.

Orchid composts

Various composts are advocated by orchid specialists when repotting an orchid – several are suggested on page 37. They must be well drained and aerated, yet retain moisture and a supply of plant foods. They must also support the plant.

HOW TO REPOT AN ORCHID

1 *Repot your orchid when the pot is congested with roots. Some orchids (Cymbidiums) have thick roots that push the plant out of its pot.*

2 *Water the compost. The following day, remove the pot. Check the roots: if old and dead, trim them off with a sharp knife or secateurs.*

3 *Choose a clean, slightly larger pot and place a 2–2.5 cm (¾–1 in) thick layer of polystyrene (plastic foam) chips in its base.*

4 *Add a small amount of compost. Then position the rootball in the pot so that its top is about 2.5 cm (1 in) below the rim of the pot.*

5 *Position the oldest part of the rootball close to one side. Add and gently firm compost. A thin stick is sometimes useful for this. Allow space for watering at the pot's top.*

6 *Stand the pot on a free-draining surface and gently fill the watering space with clean water. Allow excess water to drain away freely.*

REPOTTING INTO A BASKET

1 Orchids with cascading flowers are ideal for planting in baskets (suitable types are indicated in the A–Z of orchids on pages 46–77). Plants are usually left in baskets for several years and when being repotted can also be divided. Use secateurs to divide the plant.

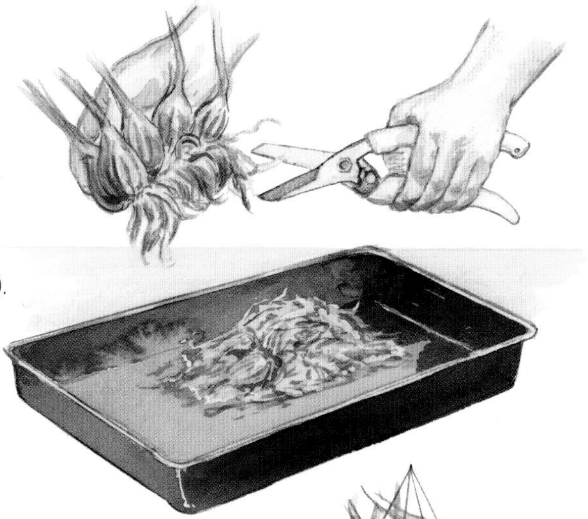

2 Use sharp secateurs to trim off dead roots and any backbulbs (old and leafless pseudobulbs).

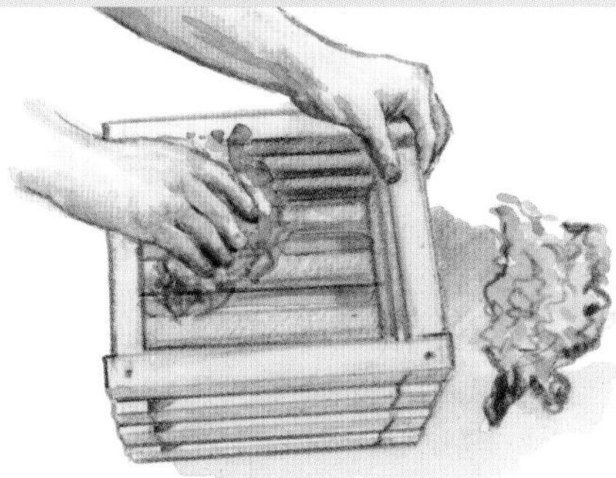

3 Line the base and sides of the basket with sphagnum moss to prevent compost falling out and to aid moisture conservation around the roots.

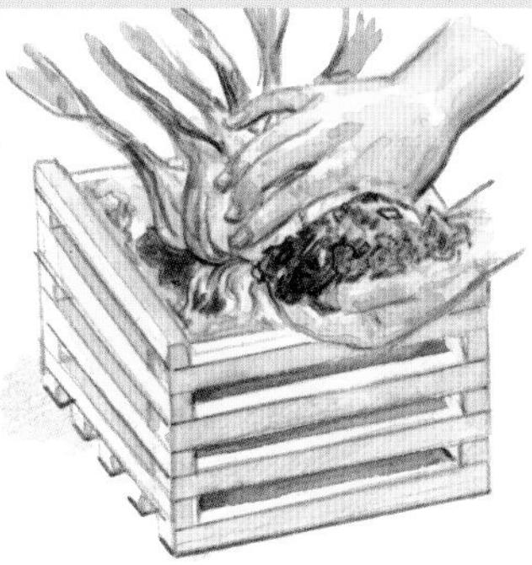

4 Hold the plant in the basket and add and firm compost around it. Suspend the basket and gently water through a rosed watering can.

5 Within a year the plant will create a magnificent display. Suspend the plant in a greenhouse where water cannot drip on plants below.

PLANTING ONTO BARK

Orchids mounted on bark, large pieces of cork or tree-fern fibre create exciting features in greenhouses. They need high humidity and therefore are not suitable for growing indoors. The bark can be secured to a wall of a lean-to greenhouse, or suspended from a hook or bracket in the roof. They can also be attached to large-mesh plastic netting.

1 Select a base (see above) and an orchid (suitable plants are indicated in the A–Z of orchids on pages 46–77). Moisten the base before use.

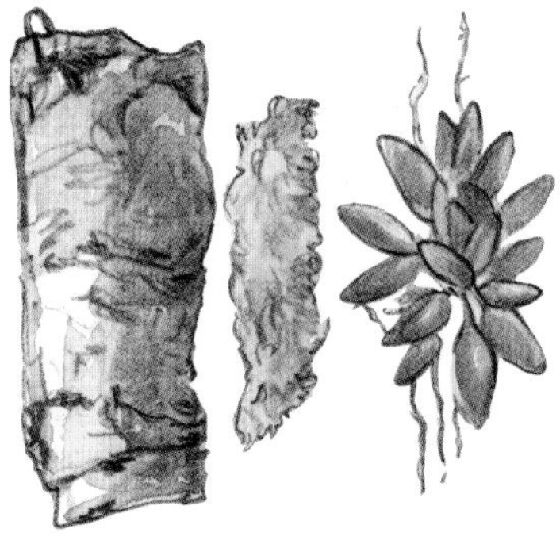

2 Form a pad of sphagnum moss or osmunda fibre and spread the roots of the orchid over it. This helps to keep them moist.

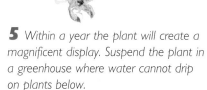

3 Use plastic-coated wire to secure the plant one-third down from the base's top. Keep the roots moist, syringe daily and feed every ten days.

Increasing orchids

Can I increase my orchids?

Orchids can be increased in several ways, but the easiest method for home gardeners is by division when plants become large and congested. Not all orchids can be increased in this way and a list of suitable ones is given below. Stem cuttings and keikis are other easy ways but, again, not all orchids are suitable – see opposite page. However, whatever the method used, always ensure that the plants you are using are healthy and free from pests and diseases.

HOW TO INCREASE ORCHIDS EASILY

Nearly all orchids can be raised from seeds, but for most home gardeners this method is far too slow and difficult. Therefore, the main choice is between division, taking stem cuttings and rooting keikis, which are small offshoots or growths that quickly develop roots. Before choosing one of these ways to increase your orchid, check which method is suitable.

INCREASING ORCHIDS BY DIVISION

The best time to divide an orchid is in spring (assuming the plant is not flowering, when it has to be delayed until flowering ceases). Plants can be divided into several parts, but each new piece should have at least three healthy pseudobulbs in leaf and signs of new growth if the plant is soon to continue creating a good display. The divided pieces can be smaller, but will take longer to create flowering plants.

Suitable orchids:

- *Anguloa*
- *Brassia*
- *Bulbophyllum*
- *Cattleya*
- *Coelogyne*
- *Cymbidium*
- *Dendrochilum*
- *Encyclia*
- *Gongora*
- *Lycaste*
- *Maxillaria*
- *Stanhopea*

After you have divided your orchid, don't expose the new plants to strong sunlight and high temperatures until their roots are established and growing strongly. Keep the compost lightly moist, but not saturated.

REPOTTING AND DIVIDING AN ORCHID

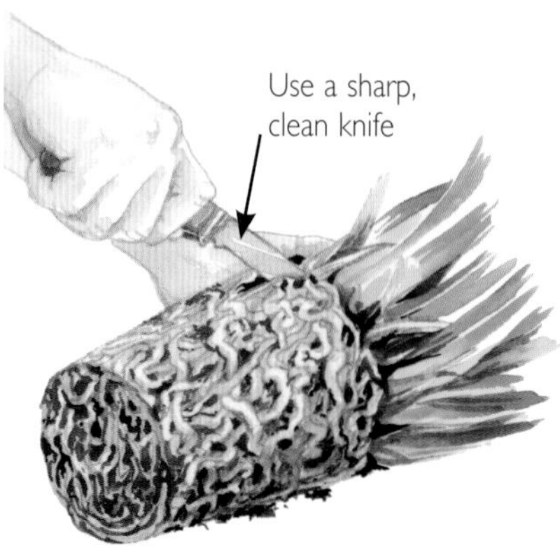

1 *Remove the plant from its pot. If the roots are very congested it may be necessary to run a knife between the pot and rootball. Use a sharp knife to cut between parts of the rootball.*

2 *Carefully divide the plant into two or three equal parts, depending on its size.*

3 *Use a sharp knife or secateurs to cut away any dead roots. Old compost usually just falls away.*

4 *Place a thick layer of polystyrene (plastic foam) chips in the base of a clean pot to conserve moisture and ensure good drainage.*

5 *Add compost and position the new plant so that the bases of the pseudobulbs are 18–25 mm (¾–1 in) below the rim; then add and firm compost.*

6 *Label and date the plant. A few days later, stand the plant on a well-drained surface and water the compost.*

TAKING STEM CUTTINGS

1 At the beginning of its growing season, use a sharp knife or secateurs to cut a 'cane' back to just above a leaf-joint (node). Take care neither to damage the parent plant nor to leave long pieces of bare stem.

2 Use a sharp knife or secateurs to cut each stem into pieces that each have at least two leaf-joints.

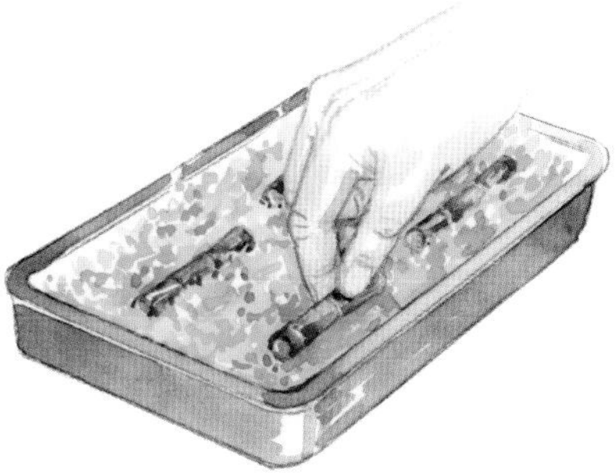

3 Fill and firm a 7.5 cm (3 in) deep tray with moist sphagnum moss and lay the cuttings on top.

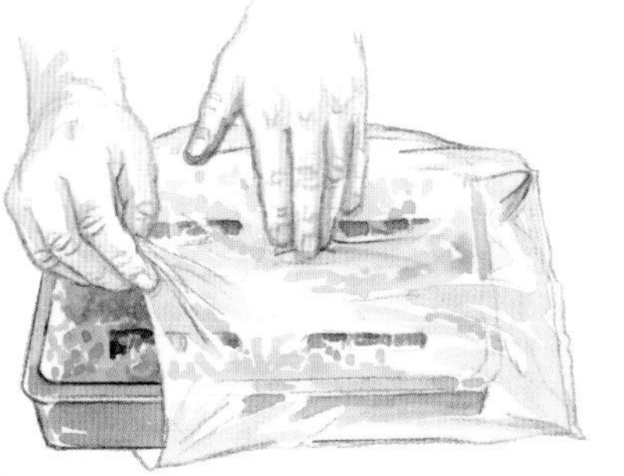

4 Lightly moisten the moss and place the tray in a clear plastic bag; place in gentle warmth and slight shade.

5 Fresh shoots will appear within 3–4 months. When rooted and with new growths, transfer them into individual pots of compost.

TAKING KEIKIS CUTTINGS

1 Keikis (adventitious growths) are said to occur when a plant is not growing strongly or has been watered too soon after a winter's rest. The day before cutting off the keikis, water the plant.

2 Use a sharp knife or secateurs to remove a keikis, taking care not to damage its stem or to reduce its roots. Young keikis usually develop new roots more easily than old ones.

3 Transfer the keikis into a pot of well-drained and aerated compost, ensuring that the stem is upright and the roots are spread out. Check that each keikis is not buried too deeply.

4 The surface of the compost should be about 12 mm (½ in) below the rim of the pot. Place the pot on a well-drained surface and gently water the compost. Then add a label and place the pot in gentle warmth.

INCREASING ORCHIDS BY KEIKIS

Some orchids develop roots from joints along their stems and during spring and summer these can be cut off and transferred to pots of compost.

Suitable orchids:
- *Dendrobium*
- *Phalaenopsis*
- *Vanda*

INCREASING ORCHIDS BY STEM CUTTINGS

Orchids that have long stems – which are often known as 'canes' – can easily be increased by cuttings. Cut the stems from the parent, trim them and insert them in pots of compost.

Suitable orchids:
- *Dendrobium*
- *Epidendrum*

Orchids that have been increased by means of stem cuttings always take longer to produce a flowering plant than those increased by division. Therefore, greater and longer care is needed during the infancy of cuttings.

Note: Orchids in each of the above propagation groups are described in the A–Z of orchids (pages 46–77).

Pests of orchids

Are orchids vulnerable to pests?

Several pests will attack orchids, but they need not become a problem if treatment is given when they are first seen. It is essential to keep all greenhouses and conservatories clean and free from rubbish and materials that might provide hiding places for pests. Clean compost and other potting materials are essential, and be sure only to buy pest-free plants. Always use proprietary insecticides that are recommended specifically for use on orchids.

Aphids

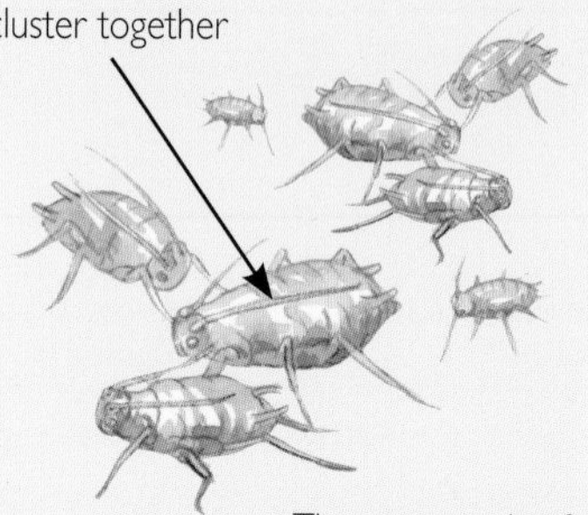
Aphids usually cluster together
They surround soft stems and shoots

Aphids, often known as greenfly, are pernicious sap-sucking pests that if uncontrolled soon spread. They usually cluster around the soft parts of shoots, especially their tips, junctions of stems and under leaves, sucking sap and causing pale areas in leaves.

Aphids are green, plumpish and may have small, short wings. As well as sucking sap and transmitting viruses from one plant to another, they excrete honeydew which attracts sooty mould (see page 44).

Greenfly are best controlled by a systemic spray that gets into a plant's tissue and directly kills sucking pests.

Rapid reproduction

Aphids are the ubiquitous pests of the plant world, especially those plants that are cultivated, grown en masse and able to provide a succulent feast of young shoots in spring and summer. Like all insects, aphids have only two interests in life – reproducing themselves and eating. As if to exacerbate the problem, at some times of the year they also have the ability to reproduce themselves at an alarming rate.

Red spider mites

Check the undersides of leaves
The mites are slow-moving and about the size of a small pinhead

Red spider mites are minute, eight-legged, spider-like creatures. They are brownish-red or straw-coloured and mainly infest the undersides of leaves, causing the upper surfaces to become speckled with yellow blotches. Severe infestations are very unsightly and leaves will often fall off the plant. If the problem is neglected, the mites will create webbing between the leaves and stems.

Red spider mites are encouraged by a dry atmosphere and are especially pernicious when plants are insufficiently watered and the compost is continually dry. Regularly mist-spraying the leaves with clean water deters infestations, while using a systemic insecticide will kill them.

Red spider mites are difficult to eradicate once they have become established.

Mites and ticks

Mites, with their eight legs, are more closely related to spiders than most other insects, which have only six legs. The range of mites is wide and as well as invading plants they will infest dogs and other animals, when often they are known as ticks.

False spider mites

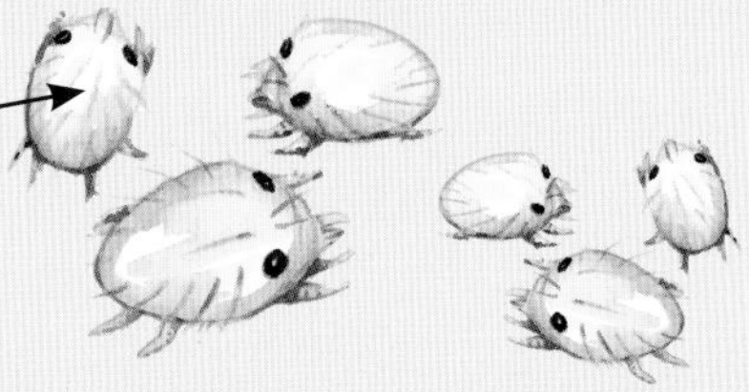
They are about the same size as red spider mites
They cause unsightly pitting in the leaves

False spider mites have, in recent years, become troublesome, especially on Phalaenopsis species. They cause pitting on the upper surface of leaves which, if left unchecked, encourages the presence of fungal diseases.

At the first sign of infestation, use the same control measures as suggested for red spider mites (see above).

Although this pernicious pest can be controlled, it leaves marks on the leaves that cannot be repaired; the plant has to grow out of the unsightliness.

Mealy bugs

Slow-moving or static pests
They resemble slightly flattened woodlice

Mealy bugs are slow-moving, eventually clustered and static creatures which resemble small, woolly, woodlice. They cluster around stems, leaf-joints and under leaves. As well as looking unsightly, they suck sap and emit sticky honeydew which encourages the presence of sooty mould (see page 44).

Small groups can be wiped off with a damp cloth or moist cotton bud. Severe infestations are difficult to eradicate and best treated with a systemic insecticide.

Scale insects

Small, flattened, scale-like discs
Wipe them off while still young

Scale insects resemble small, brown discs, usually attached to the undersides of leaves and especially along the veins. They are unsightly and cause pale spots. When young, they can be removed by wiping with a damp cloth or moist cotton bud. Heavily infested plants may also have sooty mould (see page 44). At this stage, eradication is very difficult.

The easiest way to remove them and to prevent further infestation is to use a systemic insecticide.

Thrips

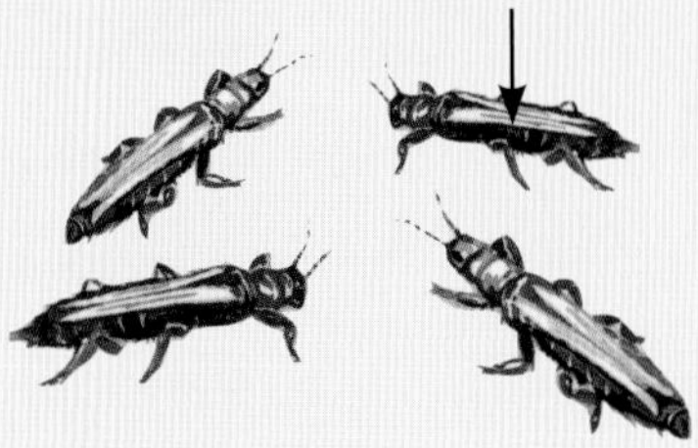
Very small quick-flying insects
They cause damage to flowers and leaves

Thrips are tiny, fast-moving and flitting, fly-like insects which feed on flowers and leaves by piercing the tissue and sucking sap. They cause silvery mottling and prevent normal leaf and flower development. Bad infestation cause stunted and unsightly plants.

Control is relatively easy, and as soon as noticed use a systemic insecticide. Because these pests rapidly move from one plant to another, be prepared to treat all of your plants.

Weevils

Wriggly, fat, legless, creamy-white grubs
Adult weevils have characteristic snouts

Weevils are pernicious pests. Adult beetles are small, not more than 12 mm (½ in) long and feed on leaves, mainly at night. The creamy-white larvae (grubs) have brown, comparatively large heads with mouth parts that are well adapted to eating roots.

The larvae live in the compost and therefore is it essential to check the compost when repotting, as well as ensuring that new plants are free from these pests. Chewed leaves are easily seen, but when larvae are present the first indication of their presence is when the foliage wilts. At this stage, the infestation is usually severe. Spray the foliage and drench the compost in an insecticide. Placing the plant in light shade helps its recovery. Avoid excessively watering the compost, which then becomes airless.

Snout beetles

Sometimes known as snout beetles, weevils are agile creatures; there are many forms, infesting a wide range of plants from vines, strawberries and apples to turnips and cabbage crops. They are widely found in gardens and often sneak into greenhouses at night. They may also infest other greenhouse plants, such as Cinerarias and Begonias.

GREENHOUSE HYGIENE

Greenhouses that are neglected may harbour pests such as woodlice, cockroaches and millipedes. These are nature's 'nasties'.

- **Woodlice** are relatively easy to eradicate, and a dusting of a general insecticide together with a thorough cleaning of the greenhouse usually gives good results.
- **Cockroaches** are nature's survivors, with nasty personal habits and an appetite for all food, although it has been claimed that they dislike cucumber and putty! Poisonous baits and other chemicals help to keep infestations under control. They mainly feed at night.
- **Millipedes** feed on roots and other underground parts of plants. They are slower moving than centipedes, which with one pair of legs on each segment are surprising agile and mainly feed on other insects. Millipedes have two pairs of legs on each segment. You can control them by removing rubbish and dusting with an insecticide.

Diseases of orchids

Are diseases common in orchids?

Several diseases attack orchids, but they need not be a problem if treatment is given when they are first seen. Viruses are also a concern, causing radical deterioration in plants and these are often transmitted by sap-sucking insects such as aphids (see page 42). When sucking sap, aphids inject plants with sap they ingested from a previously sucked plant, which may have been infected with a virus. Once present, it is near impossible to eradicate a virus.

Diseases in orchids often initially go unnoticed and therefore it is essential to check plants regularly. Carefully inspect the flowers, as well as above and under the leaves. Here are a few diseases that may affect your orchid.

Sooty mould

Sooty mould is a black fungus that grows on honeydew excreted by aphids and other sap-sucking insects, such as scale, mealy bugs and whiteflies. It does not immediately harm a plant, but makes it unsightly.

Remove the black deposit by gently wiping with a damp, soft cloth. Then, rinse off with clean, warm water. To prevent sooty mould, spray plants as soon as sap-sucking insects are seen.

Brown spot

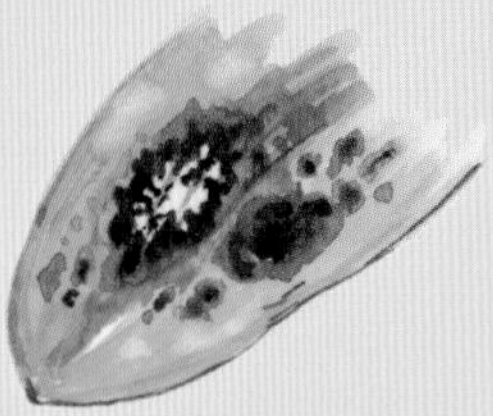

Brown spot (known in North America as brown rot) is a bacterial disease which often attacks Phalaenopsis, Paphiopedilum and Cattleya orchids. Early signs of infection are soft, watery areas on a leaf's surface, which soon become black or brown and then spread. Specifically, on Cattleya species it is usually limited to older leaves, appearing as sunken black spots. On Phalaenopsis this disease usually starts as a soft, water-soaked lesion which eventually becomes black or brown.

Infected areas should be cut out with a sharp, clean knife, and destroyed to prevent infection spreading. Dust cut surfaces with a fungicide. Once established in a collection of orchids, brown spot is difficult to eradicate.

VIRUSES

Viruses are pernicious. They are microscopic particles and their initial purpose is not to kill the plant but to use it as a host. Once a plant is infected it is difficult – if not impossible – to eradicate a virus. Eventually the plant becomes unsightly and has to be destroyed. Viruses are spread either through infected tissues when being propagated, or sap-sucking insects such as aphids. It is therefore essential to prevent infestations of insects and to buy only healthy plants.

The symptoms of viruses widely vary. With Cattleyas, for instance, as well as general debilitation irregular colouring and pale blotches appear in either the sepals or petals.

One virus, known as cymbidium mosaic virus but infesting almost all orchids, causes discoloration on leaves, which slowly become darker and sunken. On Cattleyas and Phalaenopsis it reveals itself as purplish markings which over a few weeks become brown.

Petal blight

Petal blight is a fungal disease that attacks a wide range of plants with soft tissues. In greenhouses, it is mainly caused by high humidity and results in dark brown or black spots, with pinkish edges on petals. In orchids, it mainly occurs on the early autumn flowers of Cattleya and Phalaenopsis species.

Immediately flowers are seen with this problem, remove and burn and ensure that the night-time humidity is not high. In cool situations, provide additional warmth in autumn.

Rust

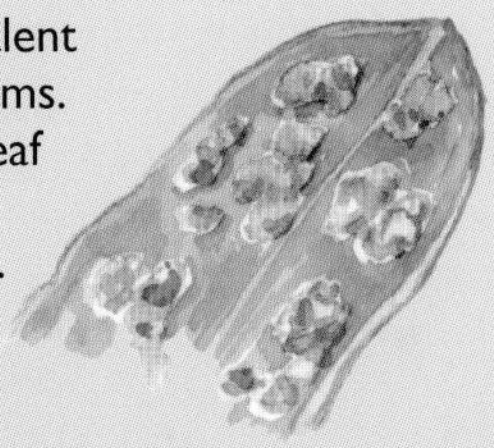

Rust is an unsightly disease and especially prevalent on Cattleyas, Epidendrums, Laelias and Oncidiums. Orange-yellow patches develop on the lower leaf surfaces, while the upper sides reveal yellow-green mottled areas directly above the patches.

It is difficult to eradicate and severely infected plants are best isolated and, eventually, destroyed. Always carefully inspect new plants.

SAFETY FIRST WITH CHEMICALS

If used carelessly, any chemicals used in the home, greenhouse or conservatory can be lethal both to families and their pets, from dogs and cats to fish and birds. Here are a few pointers that should help you avoid problems.

- Carefully follow the manufacturer's instructions. Do not be tempted to use chemicals at a higher than recommended concentration because they will not be more effective – and may even damage plants.
- Before using, check that the chemical will not damage susceptible plants. Always check that they are suitable for use on orchids.
- Do not mix two different chemicals, unless recommended to do so.
- Keep all chemicals away from children and pets. Do not transfer chemicals into bottles that children might believe to contain a refreshing drink.
- Use only chemicals recommended for indoor or greenhouse use.
- Do not allow pets to lick plants that have been sprayed. Remember that some chemicals have a residual effect for several weeks.
- When spraying indoor, remove pet birds and cover fish tanks.
- Remove all fruit and other food from a room that is being sprayed.
- Indoors, do not spray furniture or wallpapers.
- Do not use the same containers and spraying equipment for both weedkillers and insecticides.
- Thoroughly wash all spraying equipment after use, taking care not to contaminate soil or drainage ditches.

NON-FLOWERING?

If your orchid is unhealthy and growth is old and stunted, do not expect it to flower profusely – or even at all. Check that the plant is getting good light and does not need to be repotted because its roots are congested.

See pages 38–39 for repotting an orchid and pages 36–37 for watering, misting, composts and feeding.

Orchids for growing indoors and in greenhouses

Which orchids should I grow?

The range of orchids suitable for growing in greenhouses is wide and many of them can also be grown indoors. Some are excellent window plants. This A–Z of orchids encompasses a wide range of orchids, some initially introduced from the wild, while others are hybrids that have been bred by orchid specialists during the last hundred years or so. Many more hybrids are yearly added to this list.

ORCHID NAMES AND ABBREVIATIONS

In this A–Z of orchids names are given in full, but in many orchid nursery catalogues you might find the first name of the orchid abbreviated. This can be confusing to new orchid hobbyists, and therefore the following explanation might be useful. The plants in brackets after a hybrid orchid's name are those in its parentage. Not all of these orchids are discussed in this book.

Agwa = *Alangreatwoodara* (*Colax* x *Promenaea* x *Zygopetalum*)

Ascda = *Ascocenda* (*Ascocentrum* x *Vanda*)

Bc = *Brassocattleya* (*Brassovola* x *Cattleya*)

Blc = *Brassolaeliocattleya* (*Brassovola* x *Cattleya* x *Laelia*)

Burr = *Burrageara* (*Cochlioda* x *Miltonia* x *Odontoglossum* x *Oncidium*)

C = *Cattleya*

Colm = *Colmanara* (*Miltonia* x *Odontoglossum* x *Oncidium*)

Ctna = *Cattleytonia* (*Broughtonia* x *Cattleya*)

Cym = *Cymbidium*

Den = *Dendrobium*

Dtps = *Doritaenopsis* (*Doritis* x *Phalaenopsis*)

Enc = *Encyclia*

Epc = *Epicattleya* (*Epidendrum* x *Cattleya*)

Epicat = *Epicattleya*

L = *Laelia*

Lc = *Laeliocattleya* (*Cattleya* x *Laelia*)

Lctna = *Laeliocatonia* (*Broughtonia* x *Cattleya* x *Laelia*)

Milt = *Miltonia*

Mtdm = *Miltonidium* (*Miltonia* x *Oncidium*)

Mtps = *Miltoniopsis*

Oda = *Odontioda* (*Cochlioda* x *Odontoglossum*)

Odcdm = *Odontocidium* (*Odontoglossum* x *Oncidium*)

Odm = *Odontoglossum*

Odtna = *Odontonia* (*Miltonia* x *Ondontoglossum*)

Onc = *Oncidium*

Paph = *Paphiopedilum*

Phal = *Phalaenopsis*

Phrag = *Phragmipedium*

Pot = *Potinara* (*Brassavola* x *Cattleya* x *Laelia* x *Sophronites*)

Sc = *Sophrocattleya* (*Cattleya* x *Sophronites*)

Slc = *Sophrolaeliocattleya* (*Cattleya* x *Laelia* x *Sophronites*)

Vuyl = *Vuylstekeara* (*Cochlioda* x *Miltonia* x *Odontoglossum*)

Wils = *Wilsonara* (*Cochlioda* x *Odontoglossum* x *Oncidium*)

Zga = *Zygoneria* (*Neogardneria* x *Zygopetalum*)

Zygo = *Zygopetalum*

Temperatures

- Orchids can be broadly divided into the temperatures they require, such as 'cool', 'intermediate' and 'warm'. These temperature regimes are detailed on page 28.
- Within this A–Z of orchids, the temperatures best suited to the described plants are indicated.

A–Z OF ORCHIDS

The range of orchids is wide and here are many of them that are widely grown and available from garden centres and specialist orchid growers.

ANGRAECUM

Growing tips:

- Mainly grown in pots, but small plants can be mounted on pieces of bark.
- Low-light plants that need ample shade in summer and filtered light during winter.
- Water freely in summer but sparingly in winter, although the compost should not be allowed to become dry.

Angraecum eburneum

- **Easy to grow**
- **Warm temperatures**
- **Epiphytic orchid**
- **Winter-flowering**
- **Greenhouse**

Distinctive evergreen orchid with flower spikes formed of 9–12 flowers. The sepals, petals and spur are green, and with a pure white lip. The form *Angraecum eburneum superbum* has smaller but more flowers on each plant; it emits a magnificent fragrance at night.

Angraecum sesquipedale

- **Easy to grow**
- **Warm temperatures**
- **Epiphytic orchid**
- **Winter-flowering**
- **Greenhouse**

Large, evergreen orchid with leathery leaves and star-shaped, pure white flowers. Each has a long spur at its back. It is especially fragrant at night. This is the widely known Darwin Orchid, so named because when Charles Darwin, the English naturalist (1809–92), saw it he predicted the existence of a moth with a tongue long enough to reach the end of the long nectary.

ANGULOA

Growing tips:

- Grow in pots
- Shade plants, especially in summer.
- Water frequently during the growing season, but sparingly when plants are at rest in winter.

Anguloa clowesii

- **Easy to grow**
- **Cool temperatures**
- **Epiphytic orchid**
- **Early summer-flowering**
- **Greenhouse**

Large, beautiful species with tulip-like, fragrant, canary-yellow flowers. It is sometimes known as the Cradle Orchid on account of its lip, which is loosely hinged and able to rock backward and forward.

ASPASIA

Growing tips:

- Grow in a pot
- Provide light shade, especially during the summer.
- Water freely in summer, less in winter.

Aspasia lunata

- **Easy to grow**
- **Intermediate temperatures**
- **Epiphytic orchid**
- **Summer-flowering**
- **Greenhouse, indoors, windowsill**

Pretty species that bears star-shaped, brown and green flowers, each with a pinkish-white lip.

BIFRENARIA

Growing tips:

- Grow in pots or in a basket in a greenhouse.
- Grow in good light, but in summer ensure plants are shaded.
- Water freely during summer but allow the compost to dry out slightly during winter when the plant is resting. However, do not allow the compost to become totally dry.

Bifrenaria harrisoniae

- **Moderately easy to grow**
- **Cool temperatures**
- **Epiphytic orchid**
- **Summer-flowering**
- **Greenhouse, indoors**

Distinctive evergreen orchid with creamy-white flowers up to 7.5 cm (3 in) wide. The lip is covered with short, reddish-purple hairs.

BRASSIA

Growing tips:

- Grow in pots or on bark.
- Provide shade, especially in summer.
- During winter, plants need slightly less water than in summer, but the compost should not be allowed to dry out.

Brassia caudata alba 'Jem'

- **Moderately easy to grow**
- **Cool to intermediate temperatures**
- **Epiphytic orchid**
- **Summer- and autumn-flowering**
- **Greenhouse, indoors, windowsill**

Superb orchid, with graceful yellow flowers that create a very distinctive display. Plants have a compact habit and usually produce two flower sprays on each growth.

Brassia memoria Fritz Boedeker

- **Easy to grow**
- **Cool to intermediate temperatures**
- **Epiphytic orchid**
- **Summer-flowering**
- **Greenhouse, indoors, windowsill**

Distinctive evergreen hybrid with fragrant, large, spider-like, green flowers with dark brown patterning.

Brassia Rising Star

- **Moderately easy to grow**
- **Cool to intermediate temperatures**
- **Epiphytic orchid**
- **Summer-flowering**
- **Greenhouse, indoors, windowsill**

Distinctive orchid, with fragrant, spidery, red and green flowers that create a distinctive feature.

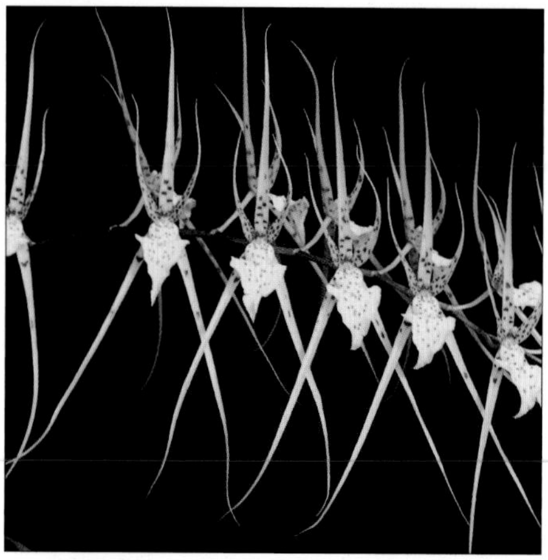

Brassia Spider's Feast 'Highland'

- **Moderately easy to grow**
- **Cool to intermediate temperatures**
- **Epiphytic orchid**
- **Summer- and autumn-flowering**
- **Greenhouse, indoors, windowsill**

Another distinctive Brassia, with long stems bearing spider-like flowers with broad, white lips.

Brassia verrucosa

- **Easy to grow**
- **Cool temperatures**
- **Epiphytic orchid**
- **Early summer-flowering**
- **Greenhouse, indoors, windowsill, growing-case**

Widely known as the Spider Orchid. The sweetly fragrant, somewhat wispy flowers, borne in graceful sprays of up to a dozen blooms, have long, thin, apple-green petals and white lips spotted in dark green. It is ideal for beginners.

x BRASSOLAELIOCATTLEYA

Growing tips:

- Grow in pots.
- Light shade, especially in summer.
- Although evergreen, plants need a rest following flowering; withhold water slightly (but still keep the compost slightly moist) and when new growth appears resume your normal watering regime.

x *Brassolaeliocattleya* Norman's Bay

- **Easy to grow**
- **Intermediate temperatures**
- **Epiphytic orchid**
- **Autumn-flowering**
- **Greenhouse, indoors, windowsill**

Evergreen hybrid that produces large, fragrant, rose-magenta flowers with frilled lips. Each flower is 20–23 cm (8–9 in) wide and the orchid is a cross between *Brassocattleya* Hartland and *Laeliocattleya* Ishtar.

x *Brassolaeliocattleya* Memoria Dorothy Bertsch 'Buttercup'

- **Easy to grow**
- **Intermediate temperatures**
- **Epiphytic orchid**
- **Summer-flowering**
- **Greenhouse, indoors, windowsill**

Superb orchid with Cattleya-type, glistening apricot-coloured flowers up to 15 cm (6 in) across. It is not a prolific flowering orchid, but each flower has a demure nature that will captivate you.

BULBOPHYLLUM

Growing tips:

- Grow in pots, on bark, or in slatted baskets.
- Light shade in summer – avoid strong and direct sunlight. In winter, give plants as much light as possible.
- Water plants well in summer but give less in winter. However, do not allow the pseudobulbs to shrivel.

Bulbophyllum careyanum

- **Moderately easy to grow**
- **Cool temperatures**
- **Epiphytic orchid**
- **Summer-flowering**
- **Greenhouse**

Distinctive orchid, often known as the Fir-cone Orchid on account of its pendent clusters of brown flowers. The flowers are fragrant.

Bulbophyllum collettii

- **Easy to grow**
- **Intermediate temperatures**
- **Epiphytic orchid**
- **Spring-flowering**
- **Greenhouse**

Attractive and unusual species with 4–6 flowers borne on each flowering spike. The overall flower colour is maroon-red, with yellow stripes. The sepals hang down, often to 13 cm (5 in).

Bulbophyllum Daisy Chain

- **Easy to grow**
- **Cool temperatures**
- **Epiphytic orchid**
- **Summer-flowering**
- **Greenhouse**

Distinctive hybrid, with heads formed of white flowers arranged like a daisy chain.

Bulbophyllum macranthum

- **Moderately easy to grow**
- **Intermediate temperatures**
- **Epiphytic orchid**
- **Summer-flowering**
- **Greenhouse**

Distinctive species, with single, white flowers, spotted purple, and borne on short stems. The lips are yellow. It is ideal for growing on bark.

Bulbophyllum vitiense

- **Moderately easy to grow**
- **Cool to intermediate temperatures**
- **Epiphytic orchid**
- **Summer-flowering**
- **Greenhouse**

Beautiful sprays of many small, pale pink flowers. It creates a distinctive display of dainty flowers.

Bulbophyllum watsonianum

- **Moderately easy to grow**
- **Cool to intermediate temperatures**
- **Epiphytic orchid**
- **Summer-flowering**
- **Greenhouse**

Beautiful species with pale pink flowers that are borne on short stems rising from the base of the plant.

CATTLEYA

Growing tips:

- Grow in pots.
- Shade plants in summer, but give good light in winter. However, do not let strong sunlight fall on the plants.
- Although evergreen, plants need a rest following flowering; withhold water slightly (but still keep the compost slightly moist) and when new growth appears resume normal watering. However, water them well during summer.

Cattleya aurantiaca

- **Easy to grow**
- **Cool temperatures**
- **Epiphytic orchid**
- **Summer-flowering**
- **Greenhouse, indoors, windowsill, growing-case**

Evergreen orchid with drooping clusters of red-orange flowers. It is often a neglected orchid because the flowers do not always open fully. However, it has the bonus of being small and well suited to small greenhouses or indoors.

Cattleya bowringiana

- **Easy to grow**
- **Intermediate temperatures**
- **Epiphytic orchid**
- **Autumn-flowering**
- **Greenhouse, indoors, windowsill, growing-case**

Evergreen, with masses – up to 20 – rose-purple flowers, each about 7.5 cm (3 in) wide. Each flower has a purple lip, marked with golden-yellow in the throat. It is an ideal orchid for a beginner.

CATTLEYA HYBRIDS TO CONSIDER

Here is a large group of hybrid Cattleyas, which are derived from many parents. There are many to choose from and in a wide colour range.

Cattleya **Abbeville 'Golden Promise'** – large, golden, sunshine-yellow, fragrant flowers during winter and into spring.

continued ...

Cattleya **Ann Komine 'Breathless'** – superbly vibrant, red, velvet-like flowers produced at various times.

Cattleya **Beaufort Gold 'Susan Fender'** – superb yellow flowers. Plants have a compact and free-flowering nature, with flowers appearing at various times.

Cattleya **Cachuma 'New Spring'** – fragrant, gentle purple flowers with yellow and darker centres during spring.

Cattleya **Caesar's Head 'Carolina Autumn'** – distinctive, with large flowers that turn bright orange as they age, with the edges assuming an intense red. It flowers during summer and into the autumn.

Cattleya **Clouds Creek 'Heavenly Scent'** – exquisitely scented orchid with white petals tinged with mauve during summer and into autumn.

Cattleya **Color Magic 'Mendenhall'** – richly coloured, yellow, fragrant flowers during autumn.

Cattleya **Drum Beat 'Heritage'** – beautiful and round, fragrant, light lavender flowers during late winter.

Cattleya **Final Touch 'Lemon Chiffon'** – compact plants with round, yellow flowers in winter.

continued ...

Cattleya **Final Touch 'Mendenhall'** – compact plant with round, apricot-orange flowers during winter.

Cattleya **Fort Watson 'Mendenhall'** – large, rich red and fragrant flowers during autumn.

Cattleya **George King 'Southern Cross'** – vigorous plant, with soft yellow, fragrant flowers in winter and into spring.

Cattleya **Goldenzelle 'Lemon Chiffon'** – beautiful light yellow, fragrant flowers. It flowers at various times.

Cattleya **Hawaiian Wedding Song 'Virgin'** – beautiful orchid with white flowers. It flowers at various times of the year.

Cattleya **Hawkinsara Koolau Sunset 'Hawaii'** – dark red, velvet-like flowers produced at various times.

Cattleya **Horace 'Maxima'** – fragrant, light lavender flowers in mid-winter.

Cattleya **Ken Battle 'Gold Crown'** – clusters of golden-yellow flowers during early spring.

continued ...

Cattleya **Lake Murray 'Mendenhall'** – superb dark red, fragrant flowers during autumn.

Cattleya **Mac Holmes 'Newberry'** – large, fragrant, dark purple flowers during summer and into autumn. It has the bonus of flowering twice a year.

Cattleya **Michael Crocker** – beautiful large, fragrant flowers produced during autumn.

Cattleya **Oconee 'Mendenhall'** – large, wine-red, fragrant flowers during summer and into autumn.

Cattleya **S.J. Bracey 'Waiolani'** – superb, burnt-orange flowers during summer and into autumn.

Cattleya **Starting Point 'Unique'** – large, fragrant, white flowers with sold purple lips during winter.

Cattleya **Susan Fender** – beautiful yellow and orange fragrant flowers with red lips. It flowers in summer and autumn.

Cattleya **Susan Fender 'Cinnamon Stick'** – large, orange, fragrant flowers produced at various times through the year.

CIRRHOPETALUM

Growing tips:

- In pots, baskets or on bark.
- Provide good light in winter, but in summer ensure that plants are shaded from direct and strong sunlight. Until established, ensure plants are shaded.
- Water well in summer, but give less than in winter; ensure that the pseudobulbs do not shrivel through lack of water.

Cirrhopetalum umbellatum

- **Moderately easy to grow**
- **Cool temperatures**
- **Epiphytic orchid**
- **Spring-flowering**
- **Greenhouse**

Evergreen and distinctive orchid with flower stems that bear up to ten flowers that are borne in a ring on short stems.

Cirrhopetalum Elizabeth Ann 'Bucklebury'

- **Moderately difficult to grow**
- **Cool to intermediate temperatures**
- **Epiphytic orchid**
- **Flowers appear at various times, but mainly during summer**
- **Greenhouse**

Evergreen orchid with distinctive pink flowers, which are mottled and have exceptionally long sepals that taper in a spider-like manner.

Cirrhopetalum Elizabeth Ann 'Jean'

- **Moderately easy to grow**
- **Cool temperatures**
- **Epiphytic orchid**
- **Autumn-flowering**
- **Greenhouse**

Distinctive, with cascading stems bearing long, white, tapering petals with fine, dark striations.

COELOGYNE

Growing tips:

- Grow in pots or baskets.
- Give full light in winter, but shade well during summer.
- It requires a resting period during winter, when the compost needs to be kept damp. Resume watering when new growth appears.

Coelogyne asperata

- **Moderate to difficult to grow**
- **Warm temperatures**
- **Epiphytic orchid**
- **Spring- and early summer-flowering**
- **Greenhouse**

Evergreen orchid with arching stems bearing spikes of 15 flowers, each about 7.5 cm (3 in) across. The large, cream-coloured flowers are very fragrant, each with an orange throat.

Coelogyne fimbriata

- **Moderately easy to grow**
- **Cool temperatures**
- **Epiphytic orchid**
- **Autumn-flowering**
- **Greenhouse, indoors, windowsill**

Short, evergreen orchid with a creeping nature and pale yellow to buff-coloured flowers with white or pale yellow lips marked dark brown.

Coelogyne barbata

- **Moderately difficult to grow**
- **Cool temperatures**
- **Epiphytic orchid**
- **Spring-flowering**
- **Greenhouse**

Evergreen, distinctive and tall orchid, with large, white sepals and petals. Additionally, the lip is bearded and with a brown fringe. When in flower it forms a tall plant, so allow plenty of space.

Coelogyne cristata

- **Moderately difficult to grow**
- **Cool temperatures**
- **Epiphytic orchid**
- **Spring-flowering**
- **Greenhouse, indoors, windowsill**

Widely grown and popular evergreen species with frost-white flowers with yellow streaks in the throat. The form *Coelogyne cristata* var. *alba* also has large white flowers, but without a yellow lip.

Coelogyne flaccida

- **Moderately easy to grow**
- **Cool temperatures**
- **Epiphytic orchid**
- **Spring- and early summer-flowering**
- **Greenhouse, indoors, windowsill**

Evergreen orchid with masses of pendent flower spikes packed with 2.5 cm (1 in) wide, ivory-white flowers. Lips are blotched with yellow and brown.

Coelogyne fuliginosa

- Moderately easy to grow
- Cool to intermediate temperatures
- Epiphytic orchid
- Autumn-flowering
- Greenhouse

Evergreen orchid, somewhat similar to *Coelogyne fimbriata*, with beautiful buff-coloured flowers with darker lips.

Coelogyne fuscescens

- Moderately easy to grow
- Cool temperatures
- Epiphytic orchid
- Autumn-flowering
- Greenhouse

Evergreen orchid with distinctive pale yellow flowers with large, deep brown lips. It usually needs a large space.

Coelogyne memoria William Micholtz 'Burnham'

- Easy to grow
- Cool temperatures
- Epiphytic orchid
- Spring-flowering
- Greenhouse, indoors, windowsill

Superb hybrid with large, pristine white flowers with bright red-orange throats. The flowers are borne in succession along a long spike. It is a cross between *Coelogyne lawrenceana* and *C. mooreana*.

Coelogyne ochracea

- Easy to grow
- Cool temperatures
- Spring- or early summer-flowering
- Epiphytic orchid
- Greenhouse, indoors, windowsill

Popular evergreen orchid with white, fragrant flowers; lips of the flowers are marked with yellow and edged in orange. There are several attractive varieties: Lemoniana has yellow flowers with lips that display pale lemon-yellow centres. It does not like excessive disturbance.

CYMBIDIUM

Growing tips:

- Grow in pots.
- Place in good light in winter, but provide light shading in summer. Strong and direct sunlight will cause scorching on the leaves.

Note: For more detailed information about growing these popular orchids, see page 20.

Cymbidium aloifolium

- Moderately easy to grow
- Intermediate to warm temperatures
- Epiphytic orchid
- Autumn-flowering
- Greenhouse

Evergreen orchid with long, pendulous stems that bear pale yellow to cream flowers, each about 36 mm (1½ in) wide. They are attractively tinged red.

Cymbidium eburneum

- Often difficult to flower
- Cool temperatures
- Epiphytic orchid
- Winter- and spring-flowering
- Greenhouse

Evergreen orchid with single or paired, large, white flowers. Each flower has a touch of yellow at its centre.

Cymbidium sanderae

- Easy to grow
- Cool temperatures
- Epiphytic orchid
- Winter-flowering
- Greenhouse

Evergreen orchid with a compact spike of white flowers. The lips are distinctively and heavily spotted in dark burgundy.

'MINIATURE' AND 'STANDARD' CYMBIDIUMS

There are both 'miniature' and 'standard' Cymbidiums. However, these terms can be misleading, with the miniature types growing to 45 cm (18 in) high and bearing flowers that are about 5 cm (2 in) wide.

'MINIATURE' CYMBIDIUMS

These flower mainly between mid-autumn and late spring, with plants remaining in flower for 6–8 weeks, and sometimes longer.

- *Cymbidium* **Aviemore 'December Orange'** – terracotta with a cream lip. Flowering during early winter.
- *Cymbidium* **Ben Venue 'Cooksbridge'** – pink flowers with a strawberry lip. Flowering during late winter and early spring.
- *Cymbidium* **Castle of Mey 'Cooksbridge Jester'** – buff-pink flowers. Flowering during early and mid-winter.
- *Cymbidium* **Castle of Mey 'Pinkie'** – delicate shell-pink. Flowering during late winter and early spring.
- *Cymbidium* **Devon Lord 'Viceroy'** – copper-coloured with chestnut overtones. Flowering during mid-winter.
- *Cymbidium* **Gleneagles 'Cooksbridge Advent'** – pink flowers. Flowering from early to late winter.
- *Cymbidium* **Gleneagles 'Cooksbridge Delight'** – small, pink flowers. Flowering during mid- and late winter.
- *Cymbidium* **Highland Wood 'Chelsea Green'** – green flowers. Flowering from late winter to late spring.

continued ...

'MINIATURE' CYMBIDIUMS continued

Cymbidium **Kings Loch 'Cooksbridge'** – green flowers with a prominent red lip. Flowering during mid- and late winter.

Cymbidium **Kintyre Gold 'Lewes'** – yellow and highlighted by a deep red band and spots on the lip. Flowering during mid- and late winter.

Cymbidium **Latigo 'Cooksbridge Sunset'** – yellowish-gold flowers with a red band on the lip. Flowering in late winter.

Cymbidium **Petit Port 'Mont Millais'** – ivory flowers with red velvet markings on the lip. Flowering from mid-winter to early spring.

Cymbidium **Sarah Jean 'Ice Cascade'** – small, white flowers. Flowering during early spring.

Cymbidium **Strathdon x Bay Sun 'Cooksbridge Wine'** – wine-pink flowers. Flowering from mid-winter through to early spring.

Cymbidium **Strathbraan 'Candy'** – creamy-white flowers suffused pink. The white lip sometimes reveals pink spots. Flowering during mid- and late winter.

Cymbidium **Strathclyde 'Lewes Fire'** – red flowers. Flowering from early to mid-winter.

'STANDARD' CYMBIDIUMS

Also known as Large-flowered Cymbidiums, 'standard' types are taller than the 'miniature' Cymbidiums and they also produce larger flowers. They flower from early winter to late spring, with the flowering period lasting for around 8–12 weeks. The range of varieties is wide and includes those plants listed below.

Cymbidium **Astronaut 'Raja'** – arching stems bearing yellow and bronze shaded flowers with a red centre.

Cymbidium **Baltic Snow** – white petals tinged yellow around their edges, with the centre red and spotted.

Cymbidium *Baltic Snow is seen here growing en masse in a greenhouse of a commercial nursery.*

Cymbidium **'Everglades Gold'** – golden-yellow, with a yellow and white centre spotted red.

Cymbidium **Goldrun 'Cooksbridge'** – yellow, with a red lip.

Cymbidium **Golden Courtier** – mainly dull yellow, with a darker centre.

Cymbidium **Highland Fair 'Cooksbridge'** – creamy-white.

Cymbidium **Lady McAlpine 'Chailey'** – white, with a crimson lip.

Cymbidium **Maureen Grapes** – green, with yellow and red centres.

Cymbidium *Golden Courtier produces large, dull yellow flowers with dark markings on the lips.*

Cymbidium *Peggy Sue has masses of dull pink flowers.*

Cymbidium **Peggy Sue** – dull pink with white edges, and predominantly deep red centres with touches of yellow and white.

Cymbidium **Pelham Grenville Wodehouse** – deep pink, with a bold red lip.

Cymbidium **Pendragon x Sachiko Promenade** – white tinged with soft red, and red and yellow-and-white centre.

Cymbidium **Red Baker** – brownish-red, with deep red centres and white and yellow touches.

continued ...

'STANDARD' CYMBIDIUMS continued

Cymbidium *Shell Pearl has gloriously coloured petals with white edges; centres are deep red, with white and yellow touches.*

***Cymbidium* Red Beauty 'Rembrandt'** – large and pink.

***Cymbidium* Shell Pearl** – striped pink with white surrounds, and deep red and yellow centre.

***Cymbidium* Sparkle 'Ruby Lips'** – green flowers with red lips.

***Cymbidium* Summer Love** – white to pale pink, with deep red centre with yellow and white.

***Cymbidium* Sylvan Candy** – white tinged mauve, and spotted mauve and white centres.

***Cymbidium* Ultimate Love 'Cooksbridge'** – distinctive green flowers.

Cymbidium *Sylvan Candy has white petals, tinged mauve; the centres are spotted with mauve and white.*

CUT-FLOWER CYMBIDIUMS

In addition to Cymbidiums grown for display in pots, some are sold through the cut-flower trade, and although flowering stems can be cut for indoor display they are occasionally offered as pot plants. There are 'miniature' and 'standard' types.

MINIATURE CUT-FLOWER CYMBIDIUMS

***Cymbidium* Artful Magic 'Martina'** – deep yellow with pink striations, and deep yellow and purple centre.

***Cymbidium* Darfield 'Eastertide'** – deep pink with white surrounds, with centres that are deep purple and white.

***Cymbidium* Earlisue 'Paddy'** – white with a hint of yellow, centre white and orange-yellow.

***Cymbidium* Florisun 'Vera'** – bright yellow with red striations, deep purple and yellow centre.

Cymbidium *Artful Magic 'Martina' has deep yellow petals with pink striations; the centres are deep yellow and purple.*

Cymbidium *Peachlet 'Irene' has blushing-pink flowers; the centres are white, tinged yellow, and spotted with purple.*

***Cymbidium* Green King 'Emerald'** – soft green, with purple and white centre.

***Cymbidium* Peachlet 'Irene'** – blushing pink, spotted purple and white tinged yellow centre.

***Cymbidium* Pistachio Mint 'Green Thumb'** – light green, with purple and yellow centre.

***Cymbidium* Summer Love 'Petra'** – white tinged pink, and centre purple and red.

STANDARD CUT-FLOWER CYMBIDIUMS

Cymbidium *Baltic Ballet 'Aida' has carmine-red flowers with deeper striations; centre is yellow and white with purple spots.*

Cymbidium *Honey Green 'Melissa' has beautiful green flowers, with striations; centre is red and white with red spots.*

***Cymbidium* Baltic Glacier 'Mint Ice'** – crisp green, with green and brown centre.

***Cymbidium* Baltic Ballet 'Aida'** – carmine-red with deeper striations, and yellow and white centre with purple spots.

***Cymbidium* Crash Landing 'Double Red'** – deep red with a hint of white, and crimson-red and white centre.

***Cymbidium* Flashpink 'Kelly'** – powder-pink with deeper striations, with deep pink and white centre.

***Cymbidium* Honey Green 'Melissa'** – green with striations, and red and white with red spotted centre.

***Cymbidium* Hot Stuff 'Ginger'** – soft green, with white centre dotted pink and purple.

***Cymbidium* Hungarian Beauty 'Freeke'** – gentle pink with striations with white surrounded, and white and yellow centre with carmine.

***Cymbidium* Saucy Etta 'Treasure'** – sunset-yellow tinged red, with yellow and deeper-red centre.

***Cymbidium* Seasons End 'Pinko'** – deep red with white edging, and white and yellow centre with deep red.

***Cymbidium* Spring King 'Showpiece'** – white, with red and yellow centre with purple dots.

***Cymbidium* Victoria Village 'Trinity'** – soft brick-red with striations, and deep red, white and yellow centre.

***Cymbidium* Yellow River 'Esther'** – bright yellow tinged pink, with yellow and deep red centre.

***Cymbidium* Yellow River 'Steffi'** – white with a tinge of pale pink, white and yellow centre deep red splodges.

Cymbidium *Spring King 'Showpiece' has white flowers; the centres are red and yellow with purple dots.*

DENDROBIUM

Growing tips:

- Grow in pots.
- Provide good light in winter, but shade in summer just sufficiently to prevent leaves and flowers being scorched.
- During winter plants need a rest, when water should be withheld until growth begins in early spring. Water well during summer.

Dendrobium delicatum

- **Moderately easy to grow**
- **Cool temperatures**
- **Epiphytic orchid**
- **Spring- and early summer-flowering**
- **Greenhouse**

Long sprays of densely packed, fragrant, creamy-white flowers borne in sprays from the top of the plant.

Dendrobium clavatum

- **Moderately easy to grow**
- **Cool temperatures**
- **Epiphytic orchid**
- **Spring- and early summer-flowering**
- **Greenhouse**

Tall orchid with clusters of bright yellow flowers which appear towards the top of the plant.

Dendrobium densiflorum

- **Easy to grow**
- **Cool temperatures**
- **Epiphytic orchid**
- **Spring- and early summer-flowering**
- **Greenhouse**

Evergreen orchid with large, pendent clusters of golden-yellow flowers. The clusters can bear 50–100 flowers.

Dendrobium farmeri

- **Easy to grow**
- **Cool temperatures**
- **Epiphytic orchid**
- **Spring-flowering**
- **Greenhouse, indoors, windowsill**

Distinctive orchid that develops pendent stems densely packed with white flowers flushed pink with yellow centres.

Dendrobium Gatton Sunray

- **Moderately easy to grow**
- **Intermediate temperatures**
- **Epiphytic orchid**
- **Summer-flowering**
- **Greenhouse**

An old and well-known evergreen orchid with loose clusters of corn-yellow flowers with a deep maroon centre on the lip. It forms a large plant and therefore does not suit all greenhouses – expect it to be about 1.2 m (4 ft) high.

Dendrobium fimbriatum

- **Moderately easy to grow**
- **Cool temperatures**
- **Epiphytic orchid**
- **Spring-flowering**
- **Greenhouse**

Distinctive species with an upright habit and sprays of golden-yellow flowers.

Dendrobium fimbriatum var. *oculatum*

- **Moderately easy to grow**
- **Cool temperatures**
- **Epiphytic orchid**
- **Spring- and summer-flowering**
- **Greenhouse**

Distinctive, with masses of golden-yellow flowers on a small plant.

Dendrobium heterocarpum

- **Moderately easy to grow**
- **Cool temperatures**
- **Epiphytic orchid**
- **Spring-flowering**
- **Greenhouse**

Eye-catching and compact species with creamy-yellow flowers that display deep brown centres.

Dendrobium miyakei

- **Moderately easy to grow**
- **Intermediate temperatures**
- **Epiphytic orchid**
- **Flowers at various times**
- **Greenhouse**

Distinctive orchid, best grown in a basket so that the trailing stems can hang freely. It bears clusters of striped, rose-pink flowers.

Dendrobium nobile

- **Easy to grow**
- **Cool temperatures**
- **Epiphytic orchid**
- **Spring-flowering**
- **Greenhouse, indoors, windowsill**

Semi-deciduous orchid with 5 cm (2 in) wide, rosy-purple petals at their tips and shading to white towards their centres. The lip reveals a rich maroon blotch in its throat. There are a couple of attractive forms, such as *Dendrobium nobile* var. Albiflorum (white with a purple throat) and *Dendrobium nobile* var. Virginale (pure white).

Dendrobium transparens

- **Easy to grow**
- **Intermediate temperatures**
- **Epiphytic orchid**
- **Spring-flowering**
- **Greenhouse**

Free-flowering species, ideal for growing on bark or in a suspended pot. You can use it to create a pretty display of white to pale rosy-mauve flowers with distinctive purple stripes.

Dendrobium wardianum

- **Easy to grow**
- **Cool temperatures**
- **Epiphytic orchid**
- **Winter-flowering**
- **Greenhouse**

Stems produce masses of fragrant, white flowers with petals, sepals and lip tipped in amethyst purple. Additionally, the lip is stained in yellow, with two maroon blotches.

Dendrobium williamsonii

- **Easy to grow**
- **Cool temperatures**
- **Epiphytic orchid**
- **Spring-flowering**
- **Greenhouse**

Compact orchid, ideal for a small greenhouse, with clusters of pale yellow flowers with bright orange lips.

DENDROCHILUM

Growing tips:

- Grow in pots or baskets
- Provide good light in winter, but light shade during summer.
- Water plants throughout the year, but less in winter when resting.

Dendrochilum cobbianum

- **Easy to grow**
- **Cool temperatures**
- **Epiphytic orchid**
- **Late winter- and spring-flowering**
- **Greenhouse, indoors**

Distinctive species with many small, fragrant, white flowers borne on drooping spikes.

Dendrochilum filiforme

- **Easy to grow**
- **Cool temperatures**
- **Epiphytic orchid**
- **Spring-flowering**
- **Greenhouse**

Pretty orchid, with small flowers borne in chains up to 30 cm (12 in) long. The yellowish-green flowers are borne close together; although each flower is not dominant, en masse they give the orchid great charm.

Dendrochilum glumaceum

- **Easy to grow**
- **Cool temperatures**
- **Epiphytic orchid**
- **Early summer-flowering**
- **Greenhouse**

Freely flowering species with small, fragrant, white flowers with orange lips.

Dendrochilum Magnum

- **Easy to grow**
- **Cool to intermediate temperatures**
- **Epiphytic orchid**
- **Late winter- and spring-flowering**
- **Greenhouse, indoors**

Distinctive orchid, with masses of small, apple-green flowers with brownish lips.

Platyclinis

Earlier, many Dendrochilum orchids were classified under the genus *Platyclinis*, and in many old books you will still see this name.

This name was frequently used in North America where, as a group, they are descriptively known as Chain Orchids.

ENCYCLIA

Growing tips:

- Grow in baskets or pots.
- Light shade is essential during summer. Provide good light in winter, but avoid strong and direct sunlight in spring.
- Plants need a winter rest, but just enough water to ensure that the pseudobulbs remain plump.

Encyclia chondylobulbon

- **Easy to grow**
- **Cool temperatures**
- **Epiphytic orchid**
- **Summer-flowering**
- **Greenhouse**

Distinctive species with upright spikes packed with thin-petalled cream flowers. The fragrant flowers have red lips.

Encyclia brassavolae

- **Easy to grow**
- **Intermediate temperatures**
- **Epiphytic orchid**
- **Summer-flowering**
- **Greenhouse**

Distinctive, handsome and tall orchid with narrow-petalled green flowers with white-cream, heart-shaped lips. Additionally, the tip of the lip is rosy-mauve. It forms a large plant and therefore needs a greenhouse.

Encyclia citrina

- **Moderately easy to grow**
- **Cool temperatures**
- **Epiphytic orchid**
- **Early summer-flowering**
- **Greenhouse**

Also known as *Cattleya citrina*, this distinctive orchid is best grown on a raft of wood or cork where it can hang down. The fragrant flowers are long lasting, with lemon-yellow flowers and a deeper yellow to the centre of the lip.

Encyclia cochleata

- **Easy to grow**
- **Cool temperatures**
- **Epiphytic orchid**
- **Flowering is sometimes continuous for up to two years**
- **Greenhouse, indoors, windowsill**

Distinctive evergreen orchid with octopus-like flowers with drooping, thin, green sepals and petals that fall beneath the rounded, dark purple or nearly black lip. Though it can flower for long periods, it usually welcomes a winter rest.

Encyclia mariae

- **Moderately easy to grow**
- **Cool temperatures**
- **Epiphytic orchid**
- **Summer-flowering**
- **Greenhouse**

Beautiful orchid, somewhat similar to *Encyclia citrina* but best grown in a pot. The highly fragrant flowers are large, with lime-green petals and sepals, and a broad, pure white lip.

Encyclia lancifolia

- **Moderately easy to grow**
- **Cool temperatures**
- **Epiphytic orchid**
- **Summer-flowering**
- **Greenhouse, indoors, windowsill**

Small, neat, summer-flowering orchid with fragrant, upright flower spikes that bear starry, 3 cm (1¼ in) wide, ivory-white flowers with red-lined lips.

Encyclia pentotis

- **Can be difficult to flower**
- **Cool to intermediate temperatures**
- **Epiphytic orchid**
- **Early summer-flowering**
- **Greenhouse**

Distinctive evergreen orchid with fragrant flowers in pairs. Each flower is creamy-white, with red lines on the lip. Small plants may be reluctant to bloom, but eventually become free-flowering.

Encyclia radiata

- **Easy to grow**
- **Cool temperatures**
- **Epiphytic orchid**
- **Summer-flowering**
- **Greenhouse, indoors, windowsill**

Evergreen orchid that bears fragrant, creamy-green flowers with red-lined lips. It flowers freely over a long period during summer and produces a very distinctive plant.

EPIDENDRUM

Growing tips:

- Grow reed types in pots. Small and creeping forms are best in small baskets or on pieces of bark.
- Provide light shade throughout summer, but less in winter.
- Water freely during summer when plants are in active growth, but less during winter.

Epidendrum Butterpatty

- **Easy to grow**
- **Cool to intermediate temperatures**
- **Epiphytic orchid**
- **Spring- and summer-flowering**
- **Greenhouse**

Distinctive hybrid, a cross between *Epidendrum paniculatum* and *Epidendrum pseudepidendrum*. It produces a wealth of green and cream flowers, each with a light yellow lip.

Epidendrum ciliare

- **Easy to grow**
- **Intermediate temperatures**
- **Epiphytic orchid**
- **Summer-flowering**
- **Greenhouse**

Pretty and showy orchid with arching sprays of large flowers with thin, green petals. The distinctive lips are white and hairy.

Epidendrum parkinsonianum

- **Easy to grow**
- **Cool temperatures**
- **Epiphytic orchid**
- **Summer-flowering**
- **Greenhouse**

Interesting orchid, with single flowers on each stem. They have pale green petals and sepal, with white lips.

Epidendrum Pink Cascade

- **Easy to grow**
- **Intermediate temperatures**
- **Epiphytic orchid**
- **Almost perpetually in flower**
- **Greenhouse**

Beautiful orchid, with clusters of creamy-pink flowers borne at the tops of tall canes. It is seldom out of flower.

GONGORA

Growing tips:

- Grow in pots or baskets.
- Provide shade during summer, but full light in winter.
- Water well in summer but sparingly in winter – just sufficient to prevent the pseudobulbs from shrivelling.

Epidendrum Plastic Doll

- **Easy to grow**
- **Cool to intermediate temperatures**
- **Epiphytic orchid**
- **Summer-flowering**
- **Greenhouse**

This is a hybrid Epidendrum, with flowers formed of green petals and sepals. Additionally, the lips are yellow and with frilled lips. The flowers are borne on the tops of upright stems.

Epidendrum pseudepidendrum

- **Moderately easy to grow**
- **Intermediate temperatures**
- **Epiphytic orchid**
- **Spring- and summer-flowering**
- **Greenhouse**

Fascinating orchid with tall, slender stems bearing loose clusters of flowers with deep green sepals and petals. Each flower has a distinctive and protruding orange lip.

Gongora galeata

- **Easy to grow**
- **Cool to intermediate temperatures**
- **Epiphytic orchid**
- **Summer-flowering**
- **Greenhouse**

Superb species, with pendent stems bearing tawny-yellow to buff-orange flowers. They have the fragrance of oranges. Additionally, *Gongora galeata* var. Alba has pale creamy-yellow flowers.

Gongora quinquenervis

- **Moderately easy to grow**
- **Intermediate temperatures**
- **Epiphytic orchid**
- **Summer-flowering**
- **Greenhouse**

Distinctive orchid that bears pendent sprays of dainty, creamy and deep red fragrant flowers.

Gongora truncata

- **Easy to grow**
- **Cool temperatures**
- **Epiphytic orchid**
- **Summer-flowering**
- **Greenhouse**

Delightful species with pendent stems bearing many small, fragrant, cream and red speckled flowers. It is ideal for growing in a basket.

LAELIA

Growing tips:

- Grow in pots, although small types are sometimes grown on bark.
- Provide shade during summer, but full light in winter.
- Water well during summer, but in winter allow the compost to almost dry out when plants are resting.

Laelia anceps

- **Easy to grow**
- **Cool temperatures**
- **Epiphytic orchid**
- **Autumn-flowering**
- **Greenhouse, indoors, windowsill**

Beautiful evergreen orchid with pale to deep rose-pink flowers. The lips are a darker shade and with yellow centres. The 10 cm (4 in) wide flowers are borne on the ends of long stems.

Laelia pulcherrima

- **Easy to grow**
- **Intermediate temperatures**
- **Epiphytic orchid**
- **Summer-flowering**
- **Greenhouse**

Distinctive evergreen orchid with large, soft-pink or white fragrant flowers.

Laelia purpurata

- **Easy to grow**
- **Intermediate temperatures**
- **Epiphytic orchid**
- **Winter-flowering**
- **Greenhouse**

Evergreen orchid, claimed to be the national flower of Brazil, with variable flowers; the narrow petals and sepals range from white to pale purple, and the lips are deep purple and frilled. Additionally, there is a white form (*Laelia purpurata* var. Alba).

x LAELIOCATTLEYA

Growing tips:

- Grow in pots.
- Shade plants in summer, but give good light in winter. However, do not let strong sunlight fall on the plants.
- Water well in summer, but less during winter – just keep the compost damp.

x *Laeliocattleya* Carrie Johnson

- **Moderately easy to grow**
- **Intermediate temperatures**
- **Epiphytic orchid**
- **Late spring-flowering**
- **Greenhouse**

Unusually coloured hybrid orchid, with cream and crimson flowers. The flowers are produced on long stems.

x *Laeliocattleya* Chitchat 'Tangerine'

- **Moderately easy to grow**
- **Intermediate temperatures**
- **Epiphytic orchid**
- **Spring- and early summer-flowering**
- **Greenhouse**

Beautiful evergreen hybrid orchid with clusters of delicate yellow-orange flowers, each about 5 cm (2 in) wide.

x *Laeliocattleya* Pomme d'Or

- **Moderately easy to grow**
- **Intermediate temperatures**
- **Epiphytic orchid**
- **Spring- and autumn-flowering**
- **Greenhouse**

Beautiful hybrid with clusters of rich yellow flowers with red veining in the throat.

LYCASTE

Growing tips:

- Grow in pots.
- Provide light shade in summer, but full light in winter.
- Water well in summer, but during winter water only to prevent the pseudobulbs shrivelling.

Lycaste cruenta

- **Easy to grow**
- **Cool and intermediate temperatures**
- **Epiphytic orchid**
- **Late winter- and spring-flowering**
- **Greenhouse**

Delightful orchid with fragrant flowers. The sepals are yellow-green, while the lip is deep golden-yellow. A deep red stain is just visible in the throat.

Lycaste skinneri

- **Easy to grow**
- **Cool and intermediate temperatures**
- **Epiphytic orchid**
- **Spring-flowering**
- **Greenhouse**

Distinctive species – although sometimes variable – with 'three-cornered' pale pink flowers. The lips are brightly coloured and create a subtle contrast with the rest of the 7.5 cm (3 in) wide flower.

Lycaste aromatica

- **Easy to grow**
- **Cool to intermediate temperatures**
- **Epiphytic orchid**
- **Winter- and spring-flowering**
- **Greenhouse**

Distinctive, with greenish-yellow sepals forming sweetly scented flowers that are up to 5 cm (2 in) wide. The lip is a bright, deep yellow.

Lycaste deppei

- **Easy to grow**
- **Cool and intermediate temperatures**
- **Epiphytic orchid**
- **Winter- and spring-flowering**
- **Greenhouse**

Large flowers with mid-green sepals spotted reddish-brown. White petals, with a yellow lip that is also spotted with reddish-brown.

Lycaste virginalis

- **Easy to grow**
- **Cool and intermediate temperatures**
- **Epiphytic orchid**
- **Late winter- and spring-flowering**
- **Greenhouse**

Delightful orchid, although with variable flowers from white, through pale to deep pink. Additionally, the lip is often spotted with crimson.

MASDEVALLIA

Growing guide:

- Grow in pots.
- Shade is needed throughout the year.
- Water carefully throughout the year but never allow the roots to become dry. Conversely, do not subject plants to excessive watering that may cause roots to decay.

Masdevallia coccinea

- **Moderately easy to grow**
- **Cool temperatures**
- **Epiphytic orchid**
- **Winter- and spring-flowering**
- **Greenhouse**

Evergreen orchid with upright stems that bear flowers which vary from lilac to deep rose.

Masdevallia angulata

- **Moderately easy to grow**
- **Cool temperatures**
- **Epiphytic orchid**
- **Spring- and summer-flowering**
- **Greenhouse**

The large flowers appear on short stems, which then hang over the side of the container. The flowers have a pale green background and are speckled all over in deep pink.

Masdevallia tovarensis

- **Moderately easy to grow**
- **Cool temperatures**
- **Epiphytic orchid**
- **Autumn-flowering**
- **Greenhouse**

Distinctive, beautiful white flowers with soft, powdery-blue undertones. They appear to have pure-white tails.

MAXILLARIA

Growing tips:

- Most are grown in pots, but those with a creeping nature in baskets or on bark.
- Provide good light, but avoid strong and direct sunlight in summer.
- Plants need a winter rest, but just enough water to ensure that the plants do not dry out completely.

Maxillaria camaridii

- **Moderately easy to grow**
- **Intermediate temperatures**
- **Epiphytic orchid**
- **Summer-flowering**
- **Greenhouse**

Sometimes listed as *Maxillaria camarardii*. Distinctive and unusual orchid with a climbing habit. The strongly scented white flowers develop from around the base of the new growth. Unfortunately, the flowers are often short-lived.

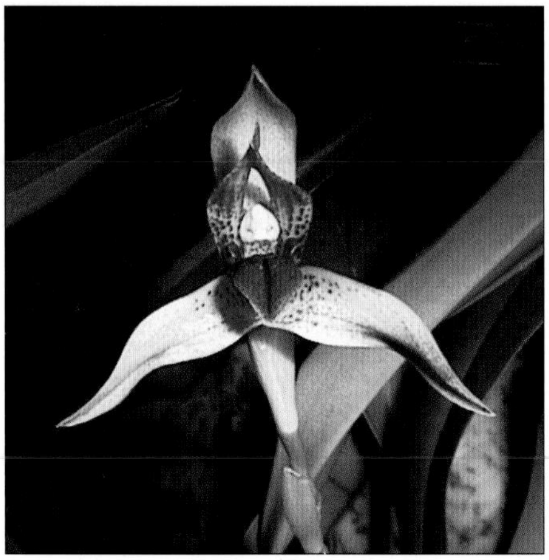

Maxillaria picta

- **Easy to grow**
- **Cool temperatures**
- **Epiphytic orchid**
- **Winter-flowering**
- **Greenhouse**

Distinctive and pretty, with masses of fragrant flowers. The insides of the petals and sepals are yellow, with reddish-brown bars on the outside that show through to the inside. The lip is creamy-white and slightly spotted red.

Maxillaria hematoglossa

- **Easy to grow**
- **Cool temperatures**
- **Epiphytic orchid**
- **Winter- and spring-flowering**
- **Greenhouses, indoors, windowsill**

Free-flowering, distinctive orchid with triangular, yellow flowers with red speckling. The lip is deep red.

Maxillaria praestans

- **Easy to grow**
- **Cool temperatures**
- **Epiphytic orchid**
- **Summer-flowering**
- **Greenhouses, indoors, windowsill**

Free-flowering orchid with yellow to reddish-brown flowers, line and dotted with dark brown. The lips are almost black. The flowers last for several weeks during summer.

Maxillaria tenuifolia

- **Easy to grow**
- **Cool temperatures**
- **Epiphytic orchid**
- **Spring- and summer-flowering**
- **Greenhouses, indoors, windowsill**

Evergreen, creeping orchid with fragrant, mainly dark or bright red flowers, 2.5 cm (1 in) wide, with yellow speckles. There is a form 'Yellow', with yellow flowers densely or lightly peppered red.

MILTONIA

Growing tips:

- Grow in pots or baskets.
- Ensure plants are shaded in summer, but less in winter.
- Water the compost throughout the year, but slightly less in winter.

Note: For more detailed information about growing these popular orchids, see page 21.

Miltonia endresii

- **Fairly easy to grow**
- **Warm temperatures**
- **Epiphytic orchid**
- **Flowering all year, but mainly in winter**
- **Greenhouse**

Also known as *Miltoniopsis warscewiczii*, this Central American orchid develops arching spikes with creamy-white sepals and petals, each with a rose-purple blotch at its base.

Miltonia clowesii

- **Fairly easy to grow**
- **Intermediate temperatures**
- **Epiphytic orchid**
- **Mainly autumn-flowering, but sometimes varied flowering times**
- **Greenhouse, indoors, windowsill**

Evergreen orchid with spectacular flowers on tall stems. The stems bear 6–10 flowers, each about 6.5 cm (2½ in) wide, reddish-brown with yellow bars. The lip is white, with a pinkish-mauve blotch on its upper part.

Miltonia roezii

- **Moderately easy to grow**
- **Intermediate temperatures**
- **Epiphytic orchid**
- **Autumn-flowering**
- **Greenhouse**

Also known as *Miltoniopsis roezii*, this pretty, Colombian orchid produces spikes bearing two or four flowers; the white petals are blotched wine-purple at their bases. The lip is white, with orange-yellow at its base.

Miltonia spectabilis

- **Fairly easy to grow**
- **Intermediate temperatures**
- **Epiphytic orchid**
- **Mainly autumn-flowering, but sometimes varied flowering times**
- **Greenhouse, indoors, windowsill**

Evergreen orchid with distinctive soft pink-white flowers. The lip is similarly coloured, but veined and blotched in mauve-purple.

MILTONIOPSIS

Growing tips:

- Grow in pots.
- Throughout the year, position plants out of strong and direct sunlight.
- Water the compost throughout the year, but slightly less in winter. Take care not to keep the compost too wet.

Miltoniopsis Anjou

- **Fairly easy to grow**
- **Cool to intermediate temperatures**
- **Epiphytic orchid**
- **Summer-flowering**
- **Greenhouse, indoors, windowsill**

Hybrid orchid with pansy-like, deep-red flowers with brown-yellow centres.

Miltoniopsis Herr Alexandre

- **Fairly easy to grow**
- **Cool to intermediate temperatures**
- **Epiphytic orchid**
- **Early summer- and autumn-flowering**
- **Greenhouse, indoors, windowsill**

Hybrid orchid with large, 10 cm (4 in) wide, white flowers with a touch of pink. Their lips are a dramatic yellow.

Miltoniopsis Hudson Bay

- **Fairly easy to grow**
- **Cool to intermediate temperatures**
- **Epiphytic orchid**
- **Summer-flowering**
- **Greenhouse, indoors, windowsill**

Hybrid orchid with a compact habit and large flowers with a creamy background and dark pink striping and blushing.

OTHER MILTONIOPSIS TO CONSIDER

Miltoniopsis *Fire Water 'Butterfly' creates a dramatic impact with its boldly coloured flowers.*

***Miltoniopsis* Emotion 4N** – deep pink with white edging, and orange-red and white centre.

***Miltoniopsis* Everest x vexillaria** – butter-yellow, with red-tinged with orange centre.

***Miltoniopsis* Fire Water 'Butterfly'** – carmine with white markings and carmine and yellow centre.

***Miltoniopsis* Hurricane Ridge 'Silvia'** – white with deep purple bases and orange centre.

***Miltoniopsis* Jean Carlson 'Desire'** – warm pink with white surround, with red and yellow centre.

Miltoniopsis *Hurricane Ridge 'Silvia' has flowers that are demure in nature.*

continued ...

OTHER MILTONIOPSIS TO CONSIDER continued

***Miltoniopsis* Jersey** – purple-pink with purple surrounded by white centre.

***Miltoniopsis* Jersey x Emotion 4N** – deep powder-pink with orange and white centre.

***Miltoniopsis* Jersey x vexillaria** – white with deep purple splashes, and orange and yellow centre.

Miltoniopsis *Lycaena 'Stamperland' has a bright-face and colour-contrasting nature.*

***Miltoniopsis* Lycaena 'Stamperland'** – white petals splashed with light purple, and light to dark orange-yellow.

***Miltoniopsis* Memoria Ida Siegal** – deep pink with purple, spider-like markings on a white base.

Miltoniopsis *Red Tide has a dramatic flower, the colours of which are intensified by strong sunlight.*

***Miltoniopsis* Red Tide** – deep pink edged white, yellow centre.

***Miltoniopsis* Saint Helier 'Pink Delight'** – deep pink striated and white edged, and deep purple centre.

***Miltoniopsis* Saint Helier 'Red Jewel'** – rich red with white and deep purple centre.

Miltoniopsis *Saint Helier 'Red Jewel' soon captures attention, especially when plants are grown en masse.*

***Miltoniopsis* Twin Peaks** – white tinged yellow, and red, orange and purple centre.

***Miltoniopsis* Zorro 'Yellow Delight'** – pale yellow with deep red and orange centre.

Miltoniopsis *Zorro 'Yellow Delight' looks attractive, even when in light shade.*

ODONTOGLOSSUM

Growing tips:

- Grow in pots.
- Provide diffused, indirect light. Take care not to expose plants, especially when they are in flower, to strong and direct sunlight.
- Water plants throughout the year, but give less during winter.

***Note:** For more detailed information about growing these popular orchids,* *see page 22.*

Odontoglossum cariniferum

- **Easy to grow**
- **Cool temperatures**
- **Epiphytic orchid**
- **Autumn-flowering**
- **Greenhouse, indoors**

Beautiful sprays of small, yellow-green flowers with brown markings. The lip is yellow and brown.

Odontoglossum Geyser Gold

- **Easy to grow**
- **Cool temperatures**
- **Epiphytic orchid**
- **Spring-flowering**
- **Greenhouse, indoors, windowsill**

Distinctive, pure golden-yellow flowers patterned with two shades of yellow.

Odontoglossum name changes

Many well-known Odontoglossums, which appeared in orchid books during previous years, have had their names changed. Here are a few of them.

O. bictoniense: now *Lemboglossum bictoniense* – yellow-green, with brown spots and a pink or white lip.

O. cervantesii: now *Lemboglossum cervantesii* – white, and marked with distinctive band of chestnut rings.

O. grande: now *Rossioglossum grande* – exceptionally popular orchid, with large, yellow flowers with bright chestnut-brown markings.

O. pulchellum: now *Osmoglossum pulchellum* – popular, with masses of small, waxy white flowers.

O. rossii: now *Lemboglossum rossii* – distinctive, with white flowers with brown markings. There is variation – some flowers are flushed pink.

OTHER ODONTOGLOSSUMS TO CONSIDER

***Odontoglossum* Costro x Nubarloo 'Lyoth Picot'** – strong red with white, frilled edging.

***Odontoglossum* Elle's Triumph** – bright sunshine-red, with deep red splodges.

***Odontoglossum* Margarete Holm** – white, with dominant sienna markings.

Odontoglossum *Margarete Holm is steeped in colour and contrast that produce a dramatic feature.*

Odontoglossum *Violetta von Holm has its colour enriched when positioned in good light.*

***Odontoglossum pescatorei* 'Lyoth Supreme'** – bridal white, with a few random red markings.

***Odontoglossum* Violetta von Holm** – brown on a white background, with red lips.

ONCIDIUM

Growing tips:

- Grow in pots, although some are suitable for growing on bark.
- Provide light shade for cool-loving orchids, but those from tropical areas (sometimes called mule-eared types) need good light throughout the year.
- Keep species plants dry during winter when growth stops; water hybrids throughout the year, but slightly less during winter.

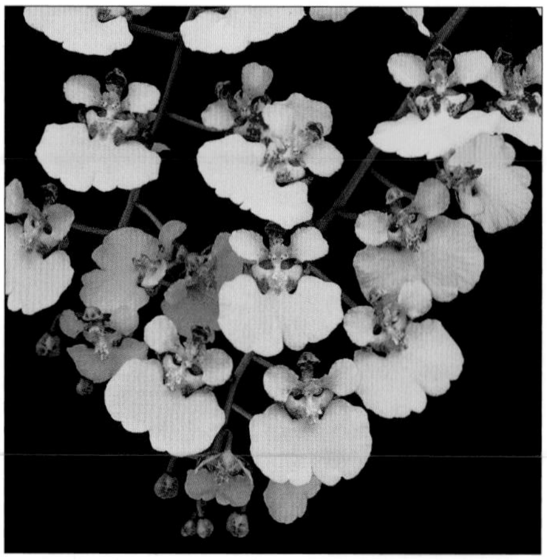

Oncidium Aloha 'Iwanaga'

- **Moderately easy to grow**
- **Intermediate to warm temperatures**
- **Epiphytic orchid**
- **Autumn- and winter-flowering**
- **Greenhouse**

Free-flowering, it produces masses of rich yellow flowers borne on several long stems.

Oncidium ampliatum

- **Easy to grow**
- **Intermediate temperatures**
- **Epiphytic orchid**
- **Spring-flowering**
- **Greenhouse**

Distinctive species, one of the Golden Shower Oncidiums and sometimes known as the Tortoise Shell orchid. It bears golden-yellow flowers in spring.

Oncidium Kitty Crocker 'Rose Giant'

- **Easy to grow**
- **Intermediate temperatures**
- **Epiphytic orchid**
- **Winter- and spring-flowering**
- **Greenhouse**

Superb hybrid, with large, soft-pink flowers. Its beauty is captivating.

Oncidium macranthum

- **Easy to grow**
- **Intermediate temperatures**
- **Epiphytic orchid**
- **Summer-flowering**
- **Greenhouse**

Well worth growing, with large golden-yellow flowers with some reddish-brown spotting on the petals.

Oncidium sphacelatum

- **Easy to grow**
- **Cool to intermediate temperatures**
- **Epiphytic orchid**
- **Autumn-flowering**
- **Greenhouse**

Develops into a large plant, with tall sprays packed with bright yellow flowers.

Oncidium ornithorhynchum

- **Easy to grow**
- **Cool temperatures**
- **Epiphytic orchid**
- **Autumn-flowering**
- **Greenhouse, indoors, windowsill**

Evergreen species orchid that produces spectacular branching and arching sprays of soft rose-lilac flowers with a yellow crest on the lip. They are fragrant and long-lasting.

Oncidium Popoki 'Mitzi'

- **Easy to grow**
- **Intermediate temperatures**
- **Epiphytic orchid**
- **Winter- and spring-flowering**
- **Greenhouse**

Superb hybrid, with spikes packed with beautiful, rich red flowers.

Oncidium Splinter 'Norman'

- **Easy to grow**
- **Cool temperatures**
- **Epiphytic orchid**
- **Autumn-flowering**
- **Greenhouse, indoors, windowsill**

Evergreen hybrid orchid with a tall growth habit and branching spikes bearing many bright yellow flowers with brown spotting.

Oncidium Star Wars

- **Easy to grow**
- **Cool temperatures**
- **Epiphytic orchid**
- **Autumn-flowering**
- **Greenhouse, indoors, windowsill**

Distinctive orchid, with tall branching spikes of small, bright yellow flowers with chestnut-brown markings.

PAPHIOPEDILUM

Growing tips:

- Grow in pots.
- Position in good but indirect light, but do not expose plants to direct or strong sunlight.
- No winter rest is needed, but give less water as the temperature falls.

Note: For more detailed information about growing these popular terrestrial orchids, see page 23.

Oncidium tigrinum

- **Easy to grow**
- **Cool temperatures**
- **Epiphytic orchid**
- **Autumn-flowering**
- **Greenhouse**

Earlier well-known and popular orchid, a parent of many superb hybrids. The fragrant flowers have yellow petals and sepals, barred chocolate-brown; the lip is bright yellow.

Paphiopedilum Delophyllum

- **Moderately easy to grow**
- **Warm temperatures**
- **Terrestrial orchid**
- **Summer-flowering**
- **Greenhouse, indoors, windowsill**

Pretty plant with mottled leaves that produces a succession of soft pink, slipper-like flowers.

Paphiopedilum insigne

- **Easy to grow**
- **Cool temperatures**
- **Terrestrial orchid**
- **Winter-flowering**
- **Greenhouse, indoors**

This orchid has been popular for many years. The petals and pouch are bronze, while the uppermost sepal is green with a white tip and spotted dark brown.

OTHER PAPHIOPEDILUMS TO CONSIDER

Paphiopedilum henryanum *has a delicacy that has attracted many orchid enthusiasts.*

Paphiopedilum henryanum – dwarf orchid, with light green petals and sepals spotted dark red. The lip is pink.

***Paphiopedilum* 'Lady Isobel'** – cream flowers streaked with brown and with a pale red lip.

***Paphiopedilum* Maudiae Vinicolor** – white with strong vertical stripes tinged red, with white and yellow centre.

***Paphiopedilum* Maudiae alba** x ***Paphiopedilum* Mystic Jewel** – beautiful green flowers striped white. Flowers are borne on tall straight stems.

Paphiopedilum micranthum – mustard-yellow with dull purple stripes, and white centre.

Paphiopedilum niveum – white splashed with faint red markings, and white and yellow centre.

Paphiopedilum *Maudiae alba* x Paphiopedilum *Mystic Jewel has an almost hypnotic quality.*

OTHER PAPHIOPEDILUMS TO CONSIDER continued

Paphiopedilum primulinum *has a brightness that is especially beautiful when highlighted by spotlights.*

Paphiopedilum primulinum – deep yellow edged with pale yellow, and yellow centre.

Paphiopedilum **Saint Isabel** – flowers striped brown on a creamy background.

Paphiopedilum **Saint Swithin** – long and twisted petals, with bold stripes on the brown and cream flowers.

Paphiopedilum tringiense – flowers boldly striped brown on a cream base.

Paphiopedilum **Yellow Tiger** – creamy-white flowers striped chocolate brown, with a raspberry-coloured pouch.

PHALAENOPSIS

Growing tips:

- Grow in pots.
- Light shading is essential, especially at the height of summer.
- Water the plants throughout the year, but take care during winter not to waterlog the compost.

Note: For more detailed information about growing these popular orchids, ***see page 24.***

Phalaenopsis 'Amaglad'

- **Easy to grow**
- **Warm temperatures**
- **Epiphytic orchid**
- **Almost perpetually in flower**
- **Greenhouse, indoors, windowsill**

This is a beautiful orchid, drenched in peach-coloured flowers with darker centres. Many flowers are clustered on each stem.

Phalaenopsis Cool Breeze

- **Easy to grow**
- **Warm temperatures**
- **Epiphytic orchid**
- **Almost perpetually in flower**
- **Greenhouse, indoors, windowsill**

Widely known as a Moth Orchid, it develops white flowers. The lip has a slight touch of yellow at its centre.

Phalaenopsis Flare Spots

- **Easy to grow**
- **Warm temperatures**
- **Epiphytic orchid**
- **Almost perpetually in flower**
- **Greenhouse, indoors, windowsill**

Beautiful orchid, with white flowers with purple speckling and crimson lips set close together on flower spikes. Each flower is about 7.5 cm (3 in) wide.

Phalaenopsis Follet

- **Easy to grow**
- **Warm temperatures**
- **Epiphytic orchid**
- **Almost perpetually in flower**
- **Greenhouse, indoors, windowsill**

Known as a Moth Orchid, it has large, handsome, pink-striped flowers. It is widely grown and is popular for indoor cultivation.

Phalaenopsis Yellow Treasure

- **Easy to grow**
- **Warm temperatures**
- **Epiphytic orchid**
- **Almost perpetually in flower**
- **Greenhouse, indoors, windowsill**

Known as a Moth Orchid, it develops primrose-yellow flowers, often with a speckling of a dark colour in the centre.

OTHER PHALAENOPSIS TO CONSIDER

Phalaenopsis *'Alice Girl' has a demure nature, with its petals contrasted by a deep red centre.*

***Phalaenopsis* 'Alice Girl'** – pink on a white background with a deep red centre.

***Phalaenopsis* Aurelia Franklin 'Golden Globe'** x ***Phalaenopsis* Aurelia Franklin 'Mendenhall'** – superb yellow flowers with slight mottling and a waxy texture.

Phalaenopsis *Aurelia Franklin 'Golden Globe'* x Phalaenopsis *Aurelia Franklin 'Mendenhall' will brighten any display.*

***Phalaenopsis* Brother Janet** – vigorous powder-pink, edged in white with deep carmine and orange centre.

***Phalaenopsis* Brother Lancer** – pale lemon, striped and speckled with pink and with deep orange lips.

***Phalaenopsis* Brother Little Yellowboy** – gentle yellow splattered with red dots, and deep red, white and orange centre.

***Phalaenopsis* ChildLine Caritas** – powdery-white, with orange centre tinged red.

***Phalaenopsis* Dragon's Charm** – green, with red splatters.

***Phalaenopsis* Fanjan's Fireworks** – beautiful flowers with dense and intricate pink veining overlaying a white background. Each flower is up to 7.5 cm (3 in) wide.

Phalaenopsis *Brother Little Yellowboy has a warm yet vibrant colour that adds a distinctive tone to any display.*

Phalaenopsis *Dragon's Charm has a medley of irregular colour splatterings that suggest the impression of a dragon.*

Phalaenopsis *Fanjan's Fireworks reveals an intricate network of veining that introduces colour dominance to displays.*

OTHER PHALAENOPSIS TO CONSIDER continued

Phalaenopsis *Golden Joy 'Lemon Stripe' has a shy nature, so ensure that it is not dominated by other orchids.*

***Phalaenopsis* 'Gold Fever'** – yellow-green, with yellow and red centre.

***Phalaenopsis* Golden Joy 'Lemon Stripe'** – soft yellow flowers with pink striping.

***Phalaenopsis* 'Golden Potential'** – yellow-green with suggestion of red dots, and white, orange and red centre.

***Phalaenopsis* Golden Treasure 'Sundance'** – golden-yellow with red vertical striations, and orange and red centre.

***Phalaenopsis* 'Hotspot'** – mottled purple on white, with deep red and white centre.

***Phalaenopsis* Malibu Debutante** – warm cream, and orange and deep red centre.

Phalaenopsis *Mary Crocker 'Newberry' has flower spikes that rise vertically, then arch gracefully.*

***Phalaenopsis* Mary Crocker 'Newberry'** – graceful plants with large, round, light pink flowers.

***Phalaenopsis* Mary Crocker 'Perfection'** – impressive, medium pink and smooth-surfaced flowers.

***Phalaenopsis* Midnight Kiss 'Newberry'** – Smooth-textured, dark pink flowers. It is extremely free-flowering and exceptionally good for growing indoors.

***Phalaenopsis* Mistral's Pixie Prelude 'Mendenhall'** – A semi-miniature type with a compact yet branching spike bearing dark pink flowers edged in white.

Phalaenopsis *Mistral's Sunrise Flame 'Tropical Sunset' introduces a new and subtle colour to an orchid display.*

***Phalaenopsis* Mistral's Sunrise Flame 'Tropical Sunset'** – with a blend of coral and pink, the flowers are sure to capture and hold your attention. Additionally, the leaves are a dark, lustrous green.

***Phalaenopsis* Mystik Golden Leopard** – beautiful yellow flowers with orange-red lips.

***Phalaenopsis* Newberry Spots** – cream with dark pink striations and spotting. Red centre.

***Phalaenopsis* Philishill** – multi-branched plant with light pink flowers splashed yellow across the lip.

Phalaenopsis *Newberry Spots is an award-winning orchid with a pattern that has a near hypnotic influence.*

OTHER PHALAENOPSIS TO CONSIDER continued

Phalaenopsis *Pink Twilight, with its well-shaped, rosy-pink flowers with darker lips, has been used to create other richly coloured and distinctive hybrids.*

Phalaenopsis **Pink Twilight** – rosy-pink, with darker lips.

Phalaenopsis **Porcelain Doll 'Mendenhall'** – superb, porcelain-white flowers which last a long time.

Phalaenopsis **Purple Valley** – deep cherry-red. They remain in flower for several months.

Phalaenopsis **'Red Oconee'** – glorious red.

Phalaenopsis **Su's Red Lip** x **Pinlong Cardinal** – bright white, with deep red centre.

Phalaenopsis *Porcelain Doll 'Mendenhall' has compact yet branching stems bearing masses of flowers.*

PHRAGMIPEDIUM

Growing tips:

- Grow in pots.
- Shade plants during summer, but in winter they need more light.
- Keep the compost evenly moist throughout the year, but take care in winter not to over-water the plants.

Praying Mantis?

In North America, Phragmipediums are widely known as Lady-slipper Orchids, in a similar way that *Cypripedium calceolus* and related species in Europe and North America are generally known as Lady's Slipper. Both are terrestrial orchids, but perhaps a more descriptive name for Phragmipediums in North America might be Praying Mantis. One variety (see page 74) has the characteristic stance of this insect.

Phragmipedium besseae

- **Moderately difficult to grow**
- **Intermediate temperatures**
- **Terrestrial orchid**
- **Summer-flowering**
- **Greenhouse**

Beautiful Phragmipedium, with three large red petals and a distinctively pouched lip.

Phragmipedium longifolium

- **Moderately difficult to grow**
- **Warm temperatures**
- **Terrestrial orchid**
- **Various flowering times**
- **Greenhouse**

Tall species, with green and cream flowers, produced over several months.

Phragmipedium pearcei

- **Moderately difficult to grow**
- **Warm temperatures**
- **Terrestrial orchid**
- **Spring- and summer-flowering**
- **Greenhouse**

Superb small orchid with pale green flowers that have darker green striping.

OTHER PHRAGMIPEDIUMS TO CONSIDER

***Phragmipedium besseae* var. D'Allesandro 'Echo' x *Phragmipedium besseae* var. D'Allesandro 'Doug Pulley'** – superbly coloured, light burnt orange flowers.

***Phragmipedium* Coffee Break 'Reachout' x *Phragmipedium* Saint Ouen 'Canary's Flight'** – large yellow flowers with long petals.

***Phragmipedium* Penn's Creek Cascade (Grande 'Gigantea' 4N x wallissi)** – long, cascading green petals. Creates a large and dominant display.

***Phragmipedium* Praying Mantis (*longifolium* x *boissierianum* 'Mendenhall')** – distinctive, with green flowers and flaring, twisting petals that give the impression of a praying mantis.

***Phragmipedium* Sorcers's Apprentice** – flowers richly shaded with green and brown.

Phragmipedium besseae *var. D'Allesandro 'Echo'* x Phragmipedium besseae *var. D'Allesandro 'Doug Pulley'.*

Phragmipedium *Praying Mantis (longifolium* x *boissierianum 'Mendenhall') is a vigorous hybrid.*

PLEIONE

Growing tips:

- Grow in shallow pans or half-pots.
- Provide light shade during summer, but full light in winter.
- Water only when in growth, from spring to autumn.

Pleione formosana

- **Easy to grow**
- **Very cool**
- **Terrestrial orchid**
- **Spring-flowering**
- **Greenhouse, indoors, windowsill**

Deciduous orchid that has been grown in alpine houses (unheated greenhouses with a good circulation of air) for many years. Now, it is often grown indoors, where it displays soft-lilac flowers. There is also a beautiful white form, with a lemon-yellow throat.

Pleione shantung 'Ridgeway'

- **Easy to grow**
- **Very cool**
- **Terrestrial orchid**
- **Spring- and early summer-flowering**
- **Greenhouse, indoors, windowsill**

A hybrid, terrestrial, deciduous orchid, derived from *Pleione formosana* and *Pleione confusa*, with large yellow and cream flowers. The lips have red markings.

Pleione speciosa

- **Easy to grow**
- **Very cool**
- **Terrestrial orchid**
- **Spring-flowering**
- **Greenhouse, indoors, windowsill**

Pretty species with mauve flowers in early spring. Each flower has yellow at the centre of the lip.

x SOPHROLAELIOCATTLEYA

Growing tips:

- Grow in pots.
- Keep plants lightly shaded during summer, but full light in winter.
- Plants need a rest following flowering; withhold water slightly (but still keeping the compost lightly moist) and when new growth appears resume normal watering.

x *Sophrolaeliocattleya* Jewel Box 'Dark Waters'

- **Moderately easy to grow**
- **Cool temperatures**
- **Epiphytic orchid**
- **Spring-flowering**
- **Greenhouse**

Superb orchid with clusters of 7.5 cm (3 in) wide, vivid crimson flowers that drench the pot in colour.

STANHOPEA

Growing tips:

- Grow in baskets.
- Provide good light throughout the year, but avoid strong sunlight at the peak of summer.
- Water plants well when they are in active growth, and slightly less at other times.

Stanhopea assidensis

- **Easy to grow**
- **Cool temperatures**
- **Epiphytic orchid**
- **Summer-flowering**
- **Greenhouse**

A superb hybrid orchid with large, pendent, beautifully scented yellow flowers with dark red spots. Sadly, the blooms are often short-lived.

Stanhopea Boileau

- Easy to grow
- Cool and intermediate temperatures
- Epiphytic orchid
- Summer-flowering
- Greenhouse

One of the few Stanhopea hybrids, with attractive but short-lived flowers during summer. Fortunately, plants make repeated flowerings throughout summer.

Stanhopea eburnea

- Easy to grow
- Cool temperatures
- Epiphytic orchid
- Summer-flowering
- Greenhouse

Also known as *Stanhopea grandiflora*, this superb species has large, fragrant, creamy-white flowers that hang from a pendent stem.

Stanhopea oculata

- Easy to grow
- Cool or intermediate temperatures
- Epiphytic orchid
- Summer-flowering
- Greenhouse

Distinctive species with exceptionally fragrant, yellow flowers borne on short, pendent spikes. The flowers have some red spotting.

Stanhopea platyceras

- Easy to grow
- Cool temperatures
- Epiphytic orchid
- Summer-flowering
- Greenhouse

Species orchid with highly fragrant yellow flowers heavily peppered in bright red and borne in pendent spikes.

Hanging-baskets

Stanhopeas are best grown in slatted hanging-baskets. This enables flower spikes to emerge unhindered from the sides and base.

Suspend the basket where the stems are able to hang freely, without being knocked or constrained.

Stanhopea tigrina

- Easy to grow
- Cool and intermediate temperatures
- Epiphytic orchid
- Summer-flowering
- Greenhouse

Widely grown species with pendent spikes bearing highly fragrant, short-lived, yellow flowers peppered in bright red.

Stanhopea wardii

- Easy to grow
- Cool and intermediate temperatures
- Epiphytic orchid
- Summer-flowering
- Greenhouse

Species orchid with large, pendent flowers that vary from pale lemon to orange, and dotted with brownish purple. Additionally, each side of the lip is blotched with velvet-purple.

Stanhopea warszewicziana

- Easy to grow
- Cool and intermediate temperatures
- Epiphytic orchid
- Summer-flowering
- Greenhouse

Also known as *Stanhopea graveolens*, this Central American orchid needs plenty of room. However, in summer it produces short-lived, strongly musk-scented, greenish-white to creamy-yellow flowers spotted maroon or purple.

VANDA

Growing tips:

- Grow in open, slatted baskets
- Good light is needed throughout the year, but avoid intensely strong sunlight at the peak of summer.
- Water freely during summer, but less in winter.

Vanda coerulea

- Moderately easy to grow
- Intermediate temperatures
- Epiphytic orchid
- Autumn- and winter-flowering
- Greenhouse

Superb species, but not widely available, with pale blue sepals and petals and a network of darker markings. The lip is purple blue and marked with white.

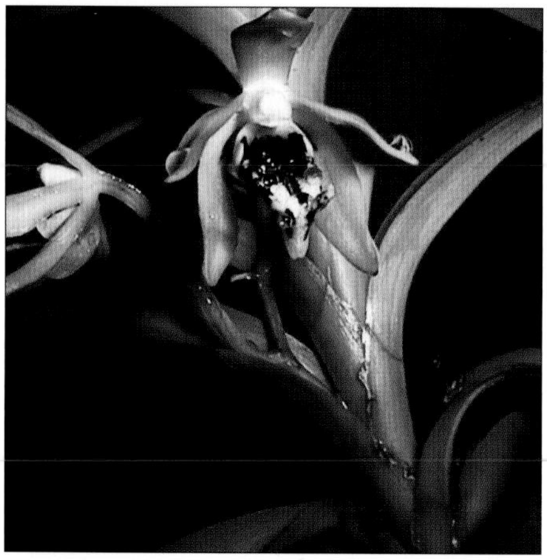

Vanda Gordon Dillon 'Lea'

- **Easy to grow**
- **Intermediate temperatures**
- **Epiphytic orchid**
- **Summer-flowering**
- **Greenhouse**

Distinctive and widely acclaimed hybrid orchid with compact spikes, bearing flowers with a white background dominantly speckled red.

Vanda Thonglor

- **Sometimes difficult to grow and flower**
- **Warm temperatures**
- **Epiphytic orchid**
- **Mainly summer-flowering**
- **Greenhouse**

Beautiful Vanda with *Vanda sanderana* in its parentage. The rose-mauve flowers are rounded, with the lower petals and sepals distinctively marked with crimson. It may flower at times other than summer.

Vanda cristata

- **Easy to grow**
- **Cool and intermediate temperatures**
- **Epiphytic orchid**
- **Early spring- to mid-summer-flowering**
- **Greenhouse, indoors**

A small species with fragrant, yellowish green flowers marked with blood-red longitudinal stripes, as well as spots.

Vanda Manuvadee 'Sky'

- **Easy to grow**
- **Cool to intermediate temperatures**
- **Epiphytic orchid**
- **Summer-flowering**
- **Greenhouse**

Beautifully and usually coloured hybrid orchid with deep purple-blue flowers.

Vanda tricolor var. *suavis*

- **Moderately easy to grow**
- **Warm temperatures**
- **Epiphytic orchid**
- **Autumn- and winter-flowering**
- **Greenhouse, indoors**

Also known as *Vanda suavis*, this fragrant, free-flowering orchid from Java and Bali has strap-like leaves and colourful flowers. The sepals are whitish-yellow, with petals barred or spotted with reddish-brown.

Vanda Robert's Delight

- **Moderately difficult to grow**
- **Intermediate and warm temperatures**
- **Epiphytic orchid**
- **Summer-flowering**
- **Greenhouse**

Hybrid orchid, a cross between *Vanda* Madame Rattana and *Vanda* Kasem's Delight, with large, bluish-purple flowers. Plants are robust and flowering is over a long period.

Vanda sanderana

- **Moderately difficult to grow**
- **Warm temperatures**
- **Epiphytic orchid**
- **Summer-flowering**
- **Greenhouse**

A superb species and often used in the breeding of other Vandas, it bears semi-erect flower spikes with soft rose to white flowers suffused with whitish pink.

x VUYLSTEKEARA

Growing guide:

- Grow in pots.
- Provide shade during summer, but give more light in winter.
- Water plants throughout the year, but give less during winter.

Hybrid parentage

x *Vuylstekeara* is a group with complex parentage. They have Cochlioda, Miltonia and Odontoglossum orchids in their ancestry and have strong similarity and growing requirements to Odontoglossums. Their main flowering time is from early winter to late spring, but this varies from one hybrid to another. One of the most attractive and widely grown hybrids is Cambria 'Plush' and this is featured on page 77.

x *Vuylstekeara* Cambria 'Lensings Favorit'

- **Easy to grow**
- **Cool/warm temperatures**
- **Epiphytic orchid**
- **Varied flowering season**
- **Greenhouses, indoors and windowsills**

A beautiful hybrid orchid with pink-blotched, red petals and sepals. The pink lip has a red central marking.

x *Vuylstekeara* Cambria 'Plush'

- **Easy to grow**
- **Cool/warm temperatures**
- **Epiphytic orchid**
- **Varied flowering season**
- **Greenhouses, indoors and windowsill**

One of the most widely grown and popular hybrid orchids, with red petals narrowly edged in white. The large lip is mainly red, with white patches and mottling. It is an ideal orchid for novices.

ZYGOPETALUM

Growing tips:

- Grow in pots or open slatted baskets.
- Provide shade throughout the year, but less so during winter.
- Water generously during summer, but less in winter.

Note: For more detailed information about growing these popular orchids, ***see page 25.***

Zygopetalum intermedium

- **Moderately easy to grow**
- **Intermediate temperatures**
- **Terrestrial orchid**
- **Winter-flowering**
- **Greenhouse, indoors**

Beautiful species orchid with flowers that strongly smell of hyacinths. It has upright flower spikes bearing 4–8 bright green flowers blotched with brown. In contrast, the lip is broad, basically white but heavily lined with purple.

Wide range of Zygopetalum hybrids

In recent years, much hybridizing has been given to Zygopetalums and this is reflected in the catalogues of orchid growers, especially in the United Kingdom as well as the rest of Europe. Many are also grown in North America. The flowers are usually characterized by bold colour and contrasts, with the petals and sepals being about equal in length.

Many new Zygopetalum hybrids were originated in Australia and are now available from orchid nurseries throughout the world. These new hybrids are free-flowering and ideal for growing either indoors or in a greenhouse. The flowers are usually highly fragrant.

OTHER ZYGOPETALUMS TO CONSIDER

***Zygopetalum* Adelaide Parklands** – lime green, white lips.

***Zygopetalum* Artur Elle 'Stonehurst'** – lime-green flowers with deep purple spotting and a purple lip.

***Zygopetalum* Kiwi Geyser 'Mendenhall'** – distinctive, superbly scented flowers with delicate veining.

***Zygopetalum* Kuitpo** – green overlaid with burnt mocha, and purple lip edged in white.

***Zygopetalum mackayi* x *Zygopetalum* (Titanic x John Banks)** – exquisitely fragrant, green and brown flowers with blue, broad lips that reveal darker stripes.

***Zygopetalum* Quorn x *Zygopetalum* Titanic 'Grand Parade'** – chocolate-black background, deep purple lip.

***Zygopetalum* Warringal Wonder** – pale olive and brown patterning, and a white lip with mauve veining.

***Zygopetalum* 'Zodiac'** – green background colour with chestnut markings and a mid-purple lip.

Zygopetalum *Artur Elle 'Stonehurst' creates a dramatic feature, whether indoors or in a greenhouse.*

Zygopetalum *Kiwi Geyser 'Mendenhall' has large, deliciously scented flowers.*

Glossary

Adventitious Usually applied to roots, but can be shoots, that arise from a position other than is normal.

Aerial roots Roots that arise from above the level of the compost.

Alliance A group of different orchids that are closely related.

Anther The part of a flower that produces pollen. An anther is borne at the top of a thin stem known as a filament and collectively forms the stamen. This is the male part of a flower.

Asymmetrical Not symmetrical and without regular shape.

Axil The upper angle between a stem or branch and a leaf.

Backbulb An old, usually leafless pseudobulb. They are seen clustered at the base of the plant and close to the new pseudobulbs.

Bifoliate Having two leaves on the same bulb.

Bigeneric A hybrid with plants of two different genera in its parentage.

Bulbous Having the character of a bulb, if not its botanical characteristics.

Cane An elongated pseudobulb.

Chlorophyll The green pigment in plants which is able, with the help of sunlight, to create growth.

Chlorotic Describes a plant with excessive yellowing.

Clones Group of plants that have been raised vegetatively from the same plant. Therefore, they are all similar.

Deciduous Losing leaves at the end of a growing season. Later, the plant will produce further leaves.

Division A method of increasing a plant by dividing the root part into two or more pieces.

Dorsal Referring to the back or outer surface and used to describe parts of flowers.

Dropping on Repotting a plant into a larger pot.

Epiphytic Describes a plant which naturally grows on another but does not derive nourishment from it, only support. Such plants are not parasites, which both live on another plant and take nourishment from it.

Hybrid A plant derived from the cross between any two unrelated parents. Such plants usually have greater vigour than normal varieties.

Inflorescence The flowering part of a plant.

Intergeneric hybrid A hybrid between two or more genera.

Internode The distance on a stem between two nodes.

Keiki A Hawaiian word for a small offshoot from a plant that can be produced naturally or by artificial means. Plants can be increased by severing and inserting these in compost.

Labellum The lip, or modified petal, of an orchid flower.

Lead An immature vegetative growth on a sympodial orchid that is able to grow into a flower-producing structure.

Lip A modified petal within an orchid flower that aids in the pollination of a flower by attracting insects or allowing insects to alight on it.

Lithophyte A plant (sometimes certain orchids) that grows on stones.

Medium The material in which an orchid is growing when in a pot, on bark or in a slatted basket.

Mericlone A plant produced by meristem culture.

Meristematic propagation A vegetative method of propagation performed under special laboratory conditions.

Monopodial Describes a plant that creates new growth from its apex or terminal bud.

Multigeneric Describes a hybrid genus containing several separate genera.

Mutation A departure from the characteristics of the parent plant, and also known as a sport.

Mycelium Microscopic fungi that must be present to enable orchid seeds to germinate.

Node A joint on a stem from which a leaf or growth starts.

Peloric Describes the abnormal formation of petals that resemble the lip.

Petal The inner part of a flower is formed of three petals; two form the lateral petals and the other the lip at the base of the flower.

Photosynthesis The growing process in plants.

Pollination The transfer of pollen from the male anther to the female stigma.

Pseudobulb A thickened portion of a stem which is able to store water and nutrients.

Raceme An unbranched inflorescence of stalked flowers.

Rhizome A horizontal, root-like stem which, in orchids, is on or just below the surface of the compost.

Sepal The outer whorl of a flower which is formed of modified leaves.

Sequential flowering Describes plants that do not produce all their flowers at the same time.

Species A classification of closely related plants.

Spike A type of inflorescence, in which the flowers do not have stems.

Stamen The male part of a flower.

Stigma The female part of a flower onto which pollen (transferred from the male part) is deposited during the act of pollination.

Sympodial Describes the way in which new shoots develop from the base of previous growths, or from pseudobulbs.

Systemic Usually refers to a chemical which enters a plant's tissue and makes it poisonous to insects.

Terrestrial Growing in soil at ground level.

Tessellation Mottling effect on leaves or flowers.

Transpiration The loss of moisture from a plant.

Unifoliate Usually applied to members of the Cattleya alliance, indicating that they bear a single leaf on each pseudobulb.

Index

Acknowledgments

AG&G Books would like to thank the following Orchid growers for their contribution: ***Carter and Holmes Orchids***, 629 Mendenhall Road, Post Office Box 668, Newberry, South Carolina 29108, USA, ***Floricultura***, P. O. Box 17, Cruquiusweg 9, 2100 AA Heemstede, Holland, ***McBeans Orchids Ltd***, Cooksbridge, Lewes, East Sussex, BN8 4PR, UK and ***Ray Creek (Orchids)***, 7 Jacklin Lane, Luddington, Scunthorpe, Nth. Lincs, DN17 4RB, UK. Photographs: AG&G Books, McBeans Orchids Ltd (front of cover and pages 2, 3B, 9TL, 11TR, 12, 14, 16, 31, 34 and 71TL), Carter and Holmes Orchids (back of cover and pages 4, 18, 27TL, 47, 48TL AND BR, 49BR, 50–52, 53T, 58TR AND BC, 68, 69BL AND BR, 70T, 71CL, 72, 73TR, 74, 75BL, 77BR), Floricultura (pages 20, 21, 24, 55–57, 65, 66TR, BL AND BR, 67, 70BL AND BC, 71TR, CR AND BR, 73TL and 76BR) and Ray Creek (pages 3TC AND TR, 5, 9TR, 11BC, 22, 23, 25, 27 EXCEPT TL, 28, 29, 30, 32, 35, 48TC, 49TR AND BL, 53B, 58BL, 59, 60–61, 62, 64, 66TL, 69TR, 73CR, 75TL, 76TL and 77TL AND BC).